CLEAN

CODE

A Comprehensive Beginner's Guide to Learn the Realms of Clean Code From A-Z

ELIJAH LEWIS

TABLE OF CONTENTS

TABLE OF CONTENTS

Introduction

Applications are available in smartphones everywhere around us. Nowadays, around 5 billion people in the world use smartphones. A huge population uses mobile phones to make the use of different applications that are available on the application store. The applications consist of different kinds of programs that utilize different coding practices. The 21st century introduced the latest innovation of smartphones in different kinds of applications. In the early years, only a few programming languages were available, and there was not a lot of innovation present regarding the programming languages.

The concept of coding was introduced in the 1950s and is still in use today with many different innovations and inventions in the concepts of programming languages. In the beginning, only some languages that were used for programming were present. These programming languages included Fortran, Cobol, and LISP technology. These technologies ruled the computer world during the 1960s. In the 1960s, the concept of gaming was introduced in simple phones. In that time, there was a concept known as ARPANET. This concept was the predecessor of the latest Internet technology, which was introduced in the 1980s. In the 1970s, different kinds of high-level programming languages were introduced. The Pascal language was introduced in the 1970s. This language is still used in the Skype software (Admin, 2018).

During the 1990s and at the beginning of the 21st century, different kinds of programming languages such as Java, C sharp, web-based technologies, etc. were introduced. These programming languages also introduced different kinds of IDE's, which are special environments used for the compilation of different kinds of code. Therefore, by using different kinds of platforms and application development tools, the process of coding was facilitated and made easier for different kinds of applications and software developers. This innovation is continuous, and every day new programming techniques are introduced to facilitate the software development process.

The coding process is a very important aspect of an application. Without coding, an application cannot be made. The coding involves different kinds of programming languages that make the structure of the application or software. Without a coding language, an application cannot be produced. The programming concepts are improved regularly and periodically. Different kinds of native platforms use native programming languages and native programming techniques. There are different components of a program that are involved in making a program complete. These components include a graphical user interface, a front end, a back end, and the databases, etc. to make the application successful. Sometimes the software also uses different kinds of 3rd party integrations to facilitate the user of the application with extended functionalities. Once when the process of programming software is complete, then different kinds of techniques are applied for improving the efficiency and performance of the program. The application development and software development are a highly innovative process because it includes a keen eye towards the design and the main goal is to fulfill the needs of the user. This book will describe all these concepts in a lot of detail, along with different pictures and diagrams to facilitate the user to understand these concepts easily.

Chapter 1

The History of Coding

The 1980s was one of the peak times of technological advancements regarding programming and coding practices. During the year 1983, the C++ language was introduced. This language is so comprehensive that it is used even nowadays. In the year 1987, Perl programming language was also introduced. This language is currently also used in Amazon, Ticketmaster, and other amazing systems. In the year 1989, the Internet was introduced. The Internet is known as one of the biggest technologies introduced until now. The Internet impacts all the digital processes in the 21st century. Different concepts, such as HTML, HTTP, and URL, were also introduced during the introductory phase of Internet development.

The 1990s are also considered as golden years regarding the coding practices. One of the most significant developments of the 1990s is the development of powerful languages such as Java, PHP, JavaScript, and Python. These languages are very important. These languages can be considered as the backbone of all modern applications and systems. Nowadays, all the social media applications, despite any platform such as Android or iOS, use these significant programming languages to achieve their processes. The Microsoft .NET system opens huge opportunities for web-based technological advancements regarding the applications. In the coming years, with the introduction of the 21st century, different innovative kinds of applications were introduced and created to facilitate the users. Even now, some of these applications are used in their advanced form to achieve the desired results.

Coding practices are innovative skills and processes. To create successful and popular applications, different kinds of applications and software developers utilize different coding abilities. The coding concept is present everywhere around us. From the process of creating different kinds of websites to creating simple formulas in the Excel spreadsheet software, it requires certain coding skills to perform the desired tasks. These applications and programs are available on the desktop, tablets, smartphones, and even in the businesses and enterprises to achieve the required business processes. Coding facilitates the smooth and efficient processing of certain tasks for the users.

What is Coding?

Coding is an essential process. Every electronic device that is available nowadays supports programs or code. It is a little confusing to understand how different devices work together. But if the structure of the electronic devices that depend on the code is broken down, the process is very easy to understand. Those people who are involved in the coding or programming processes are known as coders or programmers. The developer is also another name for the people who develop different kinds of software and systems, websites, applications, software, and different kinds of games to facilitate the users for using the latest applications and software.

The important question here is, what is a coding process? Computers or electronic devices have their own language of communication, which is known as machine code. This machine code facilitates the machines to perform different kinds of tasks. The machine language does not make a lot of sense to the general human beings. The instructions for a computer program are generally stored inside the memory. The memory is known as the storage of the computer or electronic system. Learning the machine code is a very tiring and difficult process.

Moreover, the machine code cannot be learned by the general human beings as it uses the binary language. To make things easier for human beings to understand different kinds of programming languages are introduced. The programming languages facilitate the users or human beings that are programmers to program different codes. These codes are stored inside the computer systems. These programming languages are further translated into the machine level code. In this way, the machines and other computers perform the desired functionalities. There are numerous different kinds of programming languages. The basic purpose of a programming language is very simple. The basic function of a programming language is to create the amount of code for the computers to do something.

The programmers must type what they want the compiler to do. The compiler will translate the code into the language, which is easier for the computer to comprehend and understand. When the computer understands this code, this process is called the execution of the code or the program. Coding is fundamentally known as the process of creating different kinds of computer codes to tell the computer to behave in a certain way. Every line of the program will instruct the computer to perform a certain task. A complete document that consists of different lines of codes is known as a script of the program. Every script will perform a complete function, and this function is known as a job. A common example of a script can be considered as follows:

Imagine that a user clicks the "Like" button on the application. A script is responsible for creating the action of liking the post on social media. In this way, the scripts are important to execute a proper action inside the program or an application.

The scripts of the code only do certain tasks if they are compiled in the first step and then executed in the second step. The programmers typically perform these tasks, but once when the compilation and execution are done, then the general public will be responsible for using the system. For the general people or audience to use the system, it should be converted from a script to a proper program. Once when the programmers are happy with the script of code, it is generally converted and compiled into a program. These compilation changes from the process of code to a program are understood very easily by the computer. The machine code will be stored inside a program, and everyone will use this program. The user only must download the program and use it according to his desires.

A programming language is used for coding purposes. Coding can be simple as well as complex. Different kinds of programming languages have different syntax. Different programming languages use different kinds of compilers. Numerous kinds of different libraries are involved in the programming for certain platforms. These libraries are built-in utilities that provide different kinds of functionalities to achieve the desired effects. A programmer should be well equipped with a variety of different programming techniques and a variety of different tools that are utilized in the software development process. Software is created by using a variety of different software development techniques and models.

Chapter 2

Importance of Coding

Without coding, a computer cannot properly perform its desired functionality. The coding and programming concepts are everywhere around us in this digital age. Nowadays, most of the schools are incorporating the programming languages and the necessary computer syllabus in the courses of the higher schools. The young minds are being prepared for understanding programming concepts and programming languages to become better computer professionals in the future. Coding and programming are everywhere; therefore, young minds and young students should understand the importance of it. This new change in the syllabus of the young students will enable them to understand the programming concepts right at the beginning of their educational journey. At present, most of the students are learning new techniques of how to code and understand the programming concepts in detail. Nowadays, most students have a basic understanding of computer systems and how computers perform. Programming is a very important aspect of the digital age, and therefore, it is very necessary to understand the basic programming concepts at a young age.

Programming or coding can be considered as one of the essential skills. These skills and techniques have a bright future. At present, computer knowledge and education are being incorporated at all the levels of the schools, whether the schools are government establishments or private establishments along with other science-based subjects such as mathematics, general science, physics, and chemistry. Computer education is becoming mandatory. Different kinds of electronic devices are available around us; thus, the children must be able to use the computers efficiently in the school as well as in their homes. The modern IT world requires computer education in a proper way so that the users will be more familiar with the internal workings of the system, and more and more computer knowledge will become famous. Currently, software and computer programs are becoming more and more sophisticated. Incorporating computer knowledge in the early levels of education will guide the students towards a better technology-driven future and the basic understanding regarding the computers will become stronger. The basic coding capability is one of the most desired capabilities among students at present. Some high schools made it essential for the students to be proficient in the basic coding abilities to secure a spot in high school. A large amount of money is spent on the digital environment these days. If a student has ample computer-based knowledge, then he will be able to make better decisions regarding the purchase of computer-based things online.

Coding is typically known as the process of writing different kinds of codes. A coder is the name of an individual who writes code in different programming languages. Coding is known as the form of programming, but it is used for the implementation of different computer processes involved in programming. It is the job of a coder to create communication between machines and human beings. Coders can be considered as machine language interpreters. A coder must have a complete understanding and expertise in the language which he is using to make the communication between human beings and the computer. The code is typically created in this way that the instructions are interlinked with each other, and the instructions automatically execute the commands that are to be followed next. The coding activity is further followed by the implementation of the system, debugging of the system, more testing of the system, and the quality assurance and maintenance of the system.

The instructions that the coders utilize are typically known as source code. A machine very easily understands the source code. Programming is a little different than coding. Programming is known as the method of writing several different instructions for a machine to follow, particularly. It allows different kinds of applications to run smoothly and efficiently without any internal errors. In the case of programming, the computer typically interprets the different kinds of data that are provided in the form of a program to complete a set of commands. Programmers have the duty of creating different kinds of programs. The programmers usually create the logic of a program. The logic creation part is a very innovative part of the development process, and this logic creation part requires a lot of brainstorming. Coding actually means allowing the machine to comprehend the instructions which are given by a programmer. A programmer typically creates different kinds of solutions to different kinds of problems that occur and require a solution. Becoming a successful programmer requires a lot of hard work, and usually, many years are required in the field of programming to become a better professional and to get the complete expertise of the system. Coding is a very critical process in the current age. It permits different kinds of electronic devices to be looked at the internal level. Coding is involved in every task that a machine performs. Without a proper code, a machine cannot function properly. Coding is required behind every function to perform a specific set of tasks.

When the development process is completed, different programmers convert the code and different scripts associated with the code into a single program. This program will be utilized by different individuals to get the desired functionality. The process of converting code to a program involves compiling, testing the script, debugging the script, and in the last step maintaining the quality and maintaining the system before releasing it to the public. Every application that is around us, whether it's a game or a simple website, consists of a program. There are a variety of different approaches that are utilized to learn coding techniques. A huge number of applications and websites are dedicated to the learning of the application development and software development processes. If anyone wants to understand the coding processes, a lot of knowledge is available over the Internet, and many books are also available on the subject to get a better understanding. Programming and coding are essential in the latest IT industry. Therefore, if anyone wants to be successful in this field, then he should be proficient in the programming languages and programming techniques that are utilized nowadays.

Coding involves the capability of designing, writing, testing, implementing, and maintaining a computer program source code. This code is written in the form of a computer programming language. To write a proper code, a proper understanding of the programming language is essential, and it is also essential to understand how the programs work. Sometimes, learning a programming language is a little tricky. Some languages are easier in learning than other kinds of languages. To be ready for the future, the students need to be proficient in computer programming. Nowadays, more and more businesses and corporations are migrating towards the use of technology in their processes; therefore, formal learning about essential computer programming skills is highly beneficial.

Benefits of Coding Skills

Learning about coding skills is an important skill nowadays. There are numerous numbers of benefits associated with coding skills. Learning about coding skills will benefit individuals in several different ways. Coding is an innovative field that requires imagination and creativity. When different ideas are present for creating a software system or an application, then only coding skills will be responsible for the creation of the desired system to create the system. Coding skills promote creativity in a great way. A programmer can become as creative as he can by using certain coding skills and creating the ideas of his choice and maintaining different systems. Coding skills provide several different tools that are utilized in creating the desired systems and functionalities. One common example of creativity can be considered as video games. Different software architects and designers create video games by using the tools and techniques desired for gaming creation. In this way, the designers create such innovative and captivating games that the user spends many hours playing the games without noticing the time.

If a person or an individual has a great idea, and he wants to create a system or game based on that idea, then coding skills will help to shape the system for him. Everyone has different ideas, and the coding skills allow the realization of the ideas. By using the code, a person can put the idea into a practical form. Creation is a very satisfactory process; it helps to promote innovation and it provides the opportunity of creating something new and fulfilling the dreams.

One of the basic purposes of coding or programming is to solve user problems. Different applications and systems are created to solve the real-life problems that occur in general life. One of the basic benefits of coding is that it provides problem-solving skills in an individual. By using different numbers of tools and techniques provided by the coding mechanisms, a person can solve the problems and provide great solutions to all the problems. By utilizing problem-solving skills, designing projects, and thoroughly communicating the different ideas, a person can give a deep insight into the problem, and great solutions can be created by teamwork.

Moreover, programming also offers the opportunity of testing the solution rapidly and ensuring that the system works properly or not. A person who oversees testing the software can test it immediately. When it is realized that the system is working adequately, and the problem is solved by creating the system, then the system will be released into the market. In this way, coding skills are utilized to solve real-life problems.

Typically, by using the programming and coding solving skills, a programmer or a system architect usually divides the problem into subproblems and smaller size problems. In this way, the programmer will solve the problems of users to achieve the desired results. Different kinds of situations are analyzed and measured to create a solution. The coding mechanism provides this type of breaking down the structure and getting the desired effects. Critical skills are involved in solving the problem in real life, and the programmers are given the facility to create great solutions.

After learning about the different coding techniques, a person can appreciate the working of different things. It gives a clear understanding of how different applications and software work together. This is an important factor for learning to code to appreciate the workings of computers and real-time equipment in everyday life. Learning about programming techniques give useful knowledge about solving the problems. Solving the problems is a fundamental ability that should be present in every individual to live a successful life. Learning about programming values and programming techniques is a challenging process, and it helps to create the property of resilience in people. It is a technical process. The coding also ensures that a person can return from different kinds of failure.

During the programming and coding process, different kinds of errors and bugs are encountered by different programmers. By solving these errors and issues, a person can understand that problems could be solved, and a successful system can be developed. It provides many learning opportunities to users. Software development is an innovative process in which people create applications, and they fail sometimes and then they return and learn from the mistakes. This is a great capability for learning even in real life. Learning about the coding techniques improves the capability of thinking between the individuals as a person must completely design and understand the architecture and solve the problems. Therefore, the thinking capability is increased greatly by using coding techniques.

The decomposition of the problem is one of the key features provided by the coding techniques. The decomposition technique can also be used in real life to solve other problems. Sometimes, during the application development process, a simple vague idea is the cause of the start of a real-time application. Therefore, a person can make his dream application and get immense satisfaction by using the coding techniques. The most important reason regarding the learning of programming and coding techniques is that this field will remain popular in the future. The more people learn about the coding and programming techniques, the more their future career will become bright.

Chapter 3

The Basics of Coding

This section will describe the basics of coding and programming language. Before learning any coding or programming language, it is essential to ensure that the user is aware of the basic English language. The English language is known as one of the most famous human interface languages. As the English language has its own grammar, the grammar is followed in writing the English statements properly. Without grammar, a proper sentence in the English language cannot be written. Many other human interface languages are used to communicate around the world, but in the case of programming languages, the English language is most commonly used. Every language is made up of a lot of components such as nouns, verbs, adverbs, pronouns, conjunctions, propositions, and objectives etc.

Similar to the general English language, a programming language also consists of proper rules and regulations. Programming languages contain many important elements, and these elements are several in numbers. These elements have their basics as well as advanced forms. Some of the basic elements of a programming language include a basic programming environment, which is essential for creating codes and programs. The basic syntax is essential to be followed as it defines the rules and regulations of how the language will be used. Different types of data types include the kinds of data and the variety of data that can be encountered in a programming language. Different variables need to be defined inside our programming language.

The variables are used to store a different amount of values. Keywords are known as the proper syntax or the kind of words that are used particularly, and they are particular to use for special purposes. Some basic operators are also involved in the programming language, such as the addition, minus, multiply, divide, etc. The decision-making operators help in the decision-making process in a programming language. The decision-making process includes that whether a statement is true or whether a statement is false etc. Sometimes a particular operation needs to be run again and again, and, in this case, loops are used.

Different kinds of numbers are also used in the programming language to deal with the numbers and the arithmetic operators. To store numbers or data, simple data sets known as different kinds of arrays are used. The strings are also important elements in a programming language that are used to define different characters together. Functions are also defined in a programming language. A function performs a function in a program. Different kinds of file input and output are used inside the program. The input and output file ensure that the data is well written, and the data can be read from different files or different sources. The points mentioned above just described some of the basics of elements that are used in programming languages. Different kinds of programming languages have different syntax, but all the programming languages perform similar functions. The detail of the above-mentioned basic programming elements is as follows:

- **Programming Environment**

A programming environment is highly essential for coding and programming purposes. It is the first step that needs to be followed to create a program. Before writing any code or any program, it is essential to set up the right environment for the programming purpose. The environment is a setup that needs to be set up correctly to make the working of the compiler easy. The required software setup is essential for installing the correct programming environment. The compiler or the environment setups are downloaded typically from the Internet, and they are also available from their manufacturers in the form of different CDs or disk drives. Proper installation of the programming environment is highly essential to correctly install it and then write the programs according to the programmer's needs. Nowadays, compilers and different kinds of programming environments need the computer internet connection to download some files that are available over the Internet for correctly installing the software on the computer. A web browser is also sometimes very essential to register the product over the Internet.

Sometimes without using any proper programming environment, a user can set up his own programming compiler by using the three things. These three things include a text editor that is used for creating and editing different kinds of computer programs. A compiler is needed to compile the program correctly into the library format. An interpreter is also very essential. The interpreter will be used to execute the program directly on the computer. Proper connection with the internet and a computer is desirable for using this software. Without a computer, a person cannot install anything correctly. Sometimes the users can take the help of other technically skilled individuals to set up the compilers correctly on the system.

A person should have sound technical knowledge regarding the computers and the workings of the computers to correctly install different kinds of software and applications on the computer or desktop. The correct installation of the programming environment will ensure the smooth working of the programming environment. By smoothly installing the compiler or interpreter in the computer, a person can use the software according to his desires, and the code will compile and interpret smoothly. In this case, the programmer will have more time to be spent over the workings of the application rather than worrying about the working of the compiler or the interpreter.

- **Entry Point of a Program**

The entry point of a program is known as the starting point of a program. Usually, in all the programming languages, different kinds of libraries are included, and these libraries mark the entry point of the program. Proper libraries need to be included inside a program to make the program successful. Without a proper starting point of the compiler, the compiler cannot work efficiently. Different kinds of libraries that are included in a program mark the functionality that is involved inside a program. Every program usually starts with the main () function. The main function specifies to the compiler that the compiler will start from the main point. After reading all the lines of codes available in the main function, if some functions are mentioned inside the main function, then the working of the program will move from the main statements to the functions where the pointer is pointing out. Proper format needs to be followed in the main area of the program where different function calls are present. The entry point of the program is very important in the working of the program. Everything inside the program will start from the entry point.

- **Function**

The different functions are considered as the backbone of the programs. Functions describe the set of tasks that need to be performed in a program. A program cannot function properly without different functions. Functions define the functionality that will solve user problems. Functions are primarily a small unit of the program. Every function performs a specific task. To perform every functionality, or programmer typically performs different kinds of

17

functions. Every function inside a program is unique. In almost all the programming languages, there are some predefined functions, as well as some user-defined functions. The user-defined functions are custom made functions that are designed by the programmers to achieve the desired functionality. The predefined functions have some basic set of rules and specific tasks defined inside them, and they help the programmers to save time by performing some basic tasks automatically. In the case of some other programming languages, the word "subroutine" is used instead of a function (Basics of Programming). The function of the subroutine is also the same as that of a general function. Functions are essential in the working of an efficient program.

- **Comments**

Sometimes during the working of a program, the programmers want to attach some comments. The comments will help the programmers to understand the basic functionality of the program. The comments usually do not compile during the working of the program in the compiler. The comments are one of the highlighting features of the programming language. They are user-friendly. The comments are very easy to understand. The comments will facilitate other programmers for understanding the system efficiently and effectively. For example, a programmer, when designs or creates a program he can write down the basic functionality of all the functions inside the comments. Now, when other programmers read this program, they can read the commands and understand the basic functionality of the program. The compilers entirely ignore the comments. The programmers can even write down the comments in their native languages.

- **Data Types**

Different kinds of data types are involved inside a programming language. The data types will define different kinds of data that will be used inside the program. A programming language typically facilitates a lot of data types to incorporate the requirements of several different users. Data types facilitate the working of the program according to the custom-made needs. Some data types are known as the primitive kinds of data types. These data types can be used to make more complex systems. Sometimes, some programming languages also give the facility of creating user-defined data types. Some common types of data types include character, number, long number, a small number, float, decimal number, etc. These data types are used according to the needs of the program.

- **Reserved Keywords**

Reserved keywords are known as the special keywords inside the programming language. Reserved keywords provide the reserving kind of functionality offered by special keywords. Different kinds of programming languages support different kinds of keywords. For example, the abstract keyword inside the Java programming language will make the class or function abstract. A final keyword will mark the function or variable as final, and it cannot be changed inside the program in Java programming language. The reserve key words cannot be used for other purposes inside the program. Reserve keywords greatly increase the flexibility and visibility of a program. A programmer should have ample knowledge of using the keywords effectively and efficiently inside a program.

- **Arithmetic Operators**

Most of the computer programs are used for arithmetic kinds of operations and calculations. The computing and the processing power of the computers are used for the arithmetic operations. A programmer can define many kinds of different functions, and these functions can be utilized for different kinds of programming and arithmetic needs. A computer can solve millions of calculations within a few minutes. The calculating power of a computer is very greater than the average human being. This computing power is used for solving complex arithmetic problems. Different kinds of arithmetic operators facilitate the working of different complex equations and mathematical problems. Programming languages provide several different ways to use arithmetic operators, which can be utilized according to different needs. The computing power of the computer can be greatly utilized by using proper arithmetic operators in a proper format. The low cost and high efficiency of the arithmetic processing and the computing power of the computers is one of the highlighting features used in a variety of different applications and software.

- **Relational Operators**

Relational operators are known as one of the most important operators in any programming language. These operators are used for different kinds of comparisons and contrasts between different situations and decisions. In programming, considering different kinds of variables and assigning them, different kinds of values is done very easily, but the relational operators come when the comparison needs to be determined between them. The relational operators are used with relational expressions. Relational operators can be used in their simplest forms as well as in their complex forms according to the needs of the different programs and situations. The relational operators have many kinds, but the most famous relational operators are double equal, not equal, greater than, less than, greater than or equal, less than or equal, and the not operator. These operators are typically used around with different kinds of decision statements such as the if conditions, if-else conditions, for loop, and different kinds of data relations. The relational operators greatly facilitate the relational property and the decision-making capability for a programmer between the program.

- **Logical Operators**

The logical operators are essential in any programming language and programming structure. The logical operators greatly help the decision making and certain condition making in a program. The logical operators are used to combine different results. Different kinds of conditions are checked by using the logical operators. The logical operators perform the basic logic on different kinds of statements and results. The logical operators are very important in the working of a normal program. The logical operators can be used in simple as well as different kinds of complex programs. The main kinds of logical operators are && operator, || operator and ! operators.

- **Conditional Statements**

The decision-making capability is one of the most important capabilities in any program. The decision-making capability can be considered as the basic logical essence of a program. Many situations are encountered by creating a program. A programmer must move between different kinds of options by working on a single program. Sometimes different kinds of situations are understood differently, and different options are given on a given condition. The answer to solving all these problems includes using conditional statements. The conditional statements ease and simplify the work of the programmers.

All the different kinds of programming languages include some kinds of conditional statements. The different kinds of conditional statements are also depicted in the form of a flow diagram. The flow diagrams are created in the design phase of the application development. Conditional statements are great for defining the problems in simple words. A programmer must be an expert to deal with the conditional statements for simplifying the project in detail. There are different kinds of conditional statements; the most famous

21

kind is the "if-else" statement. This structure will only work if an "if" condition is true, then the program will stop right there otherwise in case if the "if condition" will not meet the requirements, then the program will go to the else condition. Other different kinds of conditional statements include "if-else if," Switch statements, etc. The conditional statements are custom made mostly by the programmers. Usually, the programmers decide the different conditional statements and use them according to the requirements native to a particular problem.

- **Loop Structure**

Sometimes during the working of a program, particular statements need to be run again and again over a number of times. In this case, different kinds of looping structures are used by the programmers. The loops are the kinds of structures that are used by the programmers to run particular statements different numbers of times. The number of times a statement will run is based on the conditions set by the programmer. In a specific programming scenario, some loops are finite, whereas some loops are infinite. The most commonly used loops are the For loop, while loop, do-while loop, etc. The "Break" is the kind of keyword which is used to execute or terminate the statement immediately. It is usually used in a loop to stop the loop from flowing forward. Similarly, a continue statement is used to tell the compiler to continue the execution of the program in a normal way, even when the condition of a loop is met. The break statement and the continue statement are some of the most important statements used with the loops to control the flow of the program. These two statements control the flow of the normal execution of the program. The loop structure is present in almost all the programming languages.

- **Numbers**

Every programming language supports different kinds of numbers. The numbers contain a different variety of formats. A programming language should support different kinds of numbers. Different kinds of numbers are present in a programming language. The numbers include integers, floating-point numbers, decimal numbers, short numbers, long numbers, etc. The program typically must manipulate the numbers according to the needs of the program. Different keywords are used to describe different kinds of numbers. Some common keywords are int, short, long, float, etc. Every number in a programming language has a different range in which the number lies. Some numbers support the primitive data types, whereas, for some numbers, custom made data types are used. The numbers are very important in mathematical and logical operations. To use the numbers effectively, their proper format and range must be utilized. A programmer should be an expert in dealing with a variety of different numbers to make a successful and complete program.

- **Mathematical Operations Over Different Numbers**

Different kinds of mathematical functions are present within different programming languages. These functions help in mathematical calculations over large numbers. Regarding the field of mathematics, these functions play an important role. The different variety of calculations are made very simple and easy by using these built-in functions. These calculations involve the cos, sin, and tan formula calculations from trigonometry. These formulas are also utilized for calculating abstract values, square root of different numbers, absolute values of different numbers, the range between different numbers and less than or greater than values that are passed as an argument.

- **Escape Sequences**

Many different programming languages support the concept of escape sequences. The escape sequences involve a backslash character. The backslash means a special meaning for the compiler to understand. Different kinds of backslashes include inserting a new tab, inserting a backspace, inserting a new line, inserting a carriage return in the text, inserting a form field in the text, inserting a single quote character, inserting a double quote character and inserting a backslash character in the text.

- **Function**

A function is known as a block of code. A function is an organized block of code. A function is usually used for achieving custom based functionality. The main purpose of a function is to create an action. A function provides increased modularity, and it also provides a great opportunity for the code to be reused. Although many programming languages support different kinds of built-in functions but usually to deal with the needs of a program, the programmers and application developers create and maintain their own functions. All the programming languages support different kinds of functions. There are many names for functions in different programming languages. The common names for functions include methods, procedures, subroutines, etc. There are particular rules and regulations to define the functions properly. Usually, a function consists of a return type, function name, parameter list, function body, etc. The functions are called in the main area of a program. This function calling defines the use of the function in the program. Different programming languages have a different set of rules and requirements to define the functions and use them accordingly.

- **Computer Files**

The computer files are an important component of a computer. The computer files have the primary function of storing the data in a proper digital format. This format of storing the data can be in the form of text, image, or any other content type supported by the computer.

The computer files are arranged and organized in a variety of different directories present within a computer. The computer files occupy the space of the hard drive on a computer. The files are organized to keep the digital record of the content. The directories have the primary function of storing these files. During the programming phase, different programmers store their source code in the form of different extensions within the files on the computer. These files in which the source code is stored have different formats. Different programming languages have different formats of storing the data properly.

- **Input and Output Files**

The input and output processes are maintained by using the input files and output files. Typically, in common scenarios, the files are created within a computer system by using text editors. Sometimes, the programmers must generate new files by using their computer programs. File input usually means the information which is written in a file. The file output means the data, which is typically read from a file. The input and output files are usually used during the concepts of distributed computing where a client and server interact with each other, and the data is maintained within different files and directories. The concept of input and output files is also utilized during the security encryption and decryption processes.

Overview of Computer Programming

A computer program is known as a series of different instructions that are used by utilizing the different computer programming languages, and the main goal of a computer program is to solve a specific task. Two important components are very necessary for a computer program. These two components include a series of instructions and a computer programming language. Usually, a map is considered for a situation to solve a problem. The map is described in the form of different instructions, and the instructions ultimately solve the problem. Computer programs are also known as computer software. Instructions of a computer program are also known as the source code. The computer cannot work properly without a proper source code. A computer program is mandatory for the computer to perform its activities efficiently. The process of writing different kinds of computer source codes is called computer programming. Computer programs are utilized everywhere nowadays. Some very famous kinds of computer programs include MS word software, adobe software, Chrome browser, etc.

Computer Programmer

A computer programmer is also known as a computer developer. Computer programmers have the primary responsibility for creating different kinds of computer programs. The computer programs can be application programs or system programs. The system programs are native to a computer system. The system programs are responsible for booting the system and working with the operating system. A computer programmer is a skilled individual who has ample knowledge about the different programming languages as well as the different application development techniques. This knowledge helps the developer or the programmer to efficiently create new systems and solve real-life problems by using the latest technologies.

Algorithms

An algorithm in terms of programming is known as the procedure which can solve an existing problem. An algorithm is usually a step by step procedure. It is a highly effective method. An algorithm defines different kinds of valid instructions. These instructions are very properly defined and organized. At the beginning of solving a problem, a computer programmer typically writes down different kinds of steps that are required to solve a particular problem. An algorithm is not a code, but it is considered as a sketch of solving a problem. Algorithms are usually written in a crude format. This format is further refined in the next stages of the development of software. Creating different kinds of algorithms is a very innovative and brainstorming process.

Chapter 4

Famous Computer Programming Languages

There are many computer programming languages available nowadays. Among these languages, some languages are preferred, among others. Every programming language has its own advantages and disadvantages. Usually, while developing a software or a system, a programmer uses a variety of different languages and software development tools to achieve the desired effects.

Following is the detail of some famous programming languages along with their use:

- **Java**

Java is one of the most famous programming languages. This language is one of the most successful programming languages. Sun Microsystems introduced the Java programming language, and now it is owned by the Oracle. This acquisition was finalized in 2010 (Hackernoon.com, 2019). Using this language, the code for a program is written once, and this code will run everywhere. Java language supports Java virtual machines. It is a very easy language to learn. Java is a highly object-oriented language. It is one of the most robust languages. This language is very simple as compared to other programming languages. Java uses different kinds of concepts, such as memory allocation is automated, and it provides very efficient garbage collection methods. Java is used over a variety of different platforms. Java is a cross-platform application development language. The Java code is compiled into low-level machine code. The Java code is executed finally by using the J VM platform. Java is utilized as the foundation of the Android operating system. This language is very flexible. This language is favored by many beginners who want to learn the programming languages.

- **JavaScript**

JavaScript is known as one of the most widely used languages nowadays. It is almost impossible to develop anything without using the JavaScript language. It is one of the most popular languages among the programmer community. JavaScript is a very lightweight, interpreted language. It is greatly used for developing the front end of the applications. It is considered a very good language for providing a very easy way of creating web-based applications. It provides interactive and responsive web-based applications. One of the most beautiful features of the JavaScript language is that it consists of large compatibility with all the other browsers. It is a very flexible language. Sometimes Java is also used for the server-side. It is a very easy language to learn for beginners. It is a very interactive and innovative language.

- **Python**

Python is a general-purpose programming language. It is a very user-friendly language. The syntax of this language is very clear and simple. Python is an object-oriented language. It is mostly used for back end development purposes. It is easy to learn, and it provides rich features and great support for developing the applications. It is used to create different kinds of versatile and powerful applications. This language is mostly used in the areas of data science and scientific computing. Nowadays, with the advancements in the fields of machine learning and artificial intelligence, this language is mostly used in these new technological areas. It is also greatly used in engineering-based applications. It provides many different functions that are unique in their functionality, and these functions help the developers greatly. It is a simple language to use; therefore, it is favored by most of the developers nowadays.

- **C++**

This language was initially introduced in the 1970s. This language is a very popular choice, even at present. This language is used for creating high-performance applications. C++ language is the hybrid of the original C language. It is an object-oriented language. It is built over the framework of the C language. It is used for developing high-level applications and programs. It is one of the most dynamically used languages. It is executed over the real-time environments. For developing different kinds of games, computer graphics, and augmented reality-based applications, this language is used. It is one of the most usable languages, and it is a very comprehensive language.

- **PHP**

This is a general-purpose programming language. It is used for scripting purposes. This language usually runs and compiles over the server. This language is used to create different kinds of web pages which are originally created in the HTML language. It is one of the most famous languages. It is a free language. This language is very cheap in the sense that it is easier to install, and it is very easy to use. Most of the new programmers start their application development journey by using the PHP language. It provides great flexibility for creating web-based applications. A huge community of web-based developers uses the PHP language around the world. It is also used for the creation of dynamic content. It is used in many areas of application development nowadays. With the popularity of the WordPress system, PHP is used greatly in the present IT world.

- **Swift**

This language is an open-source programming language. It is a general-purpose programming language. Apple Inc developed this language. This language is designed for the development of the native applications of the Apple platform. The swift language uses the different concepts of Python and Ruby language. It is a very user-friendly language. This language is very easy to use. This language is very fast. This language is very secure, and the syntax is very easy to read. It is very easy to do the debugging in the swift language. Less amount of code is required by using swift language. Therefore, it is one of the best choices of programming language for developing different Apple operating system-based applications. The syntax of the swift language resembles the simple English language; therefore, anyone can understand the syntax easily.

- **C#**

C sharp is a relatively new language. This language is one of the most popular and powerful languages currently. This language is very object-oriented. This language is developed by Microsoft. It is most widely used in creating different kinds of desktop applications. Currently, it is also utilized for developing windows-based applications for Windows 8 and Windows 10 platforms. This language requires a .NET platform to function effectively and efficiently. A variety of different features are available in the C sharp language. This language is very easy to learn. It provides a consistent code that is smooth to learn, and it runs smoothly over different platforms. It is a very logical language. This language is very easy to use for debugging processes. The error spotting is very easy by using this language. It is a statically typed language. This language is a perfect choice for developing different kinds of desktop applications, web-based applications, and different kinds of gaming applications. This language also provides different kinds of tools, such as different desktop applications, web-based applications, and developing cross-platform applications.

- **Ruby**

This language is an open-source language. It provides a dynamic programming facility. This language is based on simplicity and productivity. The basic goal of the Ruby language is to simplify the processes of application development. It is used for full-stack web-based developments. It is a dynamic Language. It is used for higher-level application programming. The syntax of this language resembles the basic English language. Less number of lines of codes are required by using this language. This language is very easy to maintain. It is a highly flexible language.

- **SQL**

SQL is the abbreviation of structured query language. This language is used for operating with different databases. This language includes different kinds of facilities for the storage of the data, alternating the data, and retrieving the desired results, which are stored in a database. SQL works with relational databases. This language is used for organizing and securely arranging the data. The data is kept secure by using SQL operations. This language is used for maintaining the databases. This language supports the integrity of the databases. Despite any data size, this language is used to maintain the databases and integrity of the data in an effective way. SQL is one of the most widely used languages. It is used over a variety of different web-based frameworks. This language is also used in a variety of different database applications. This language expects the developers to have very strong decision-making abilities. If someone wants to become a database manager in the future, then this language is one of the prime choices to learn. SQL development is very high in demand. Different kinds of data sets are organized and arranged by using the SQL language to achieve the desired results.

Learning new languages can help programmers create different career opportunities in the future, helps them to learn new skills, and enhance their knowledge. To learn a programming language, it is essential to have a proper goal in the mind of the developer. A person should learn a programming language after knowing about its advantages and disadvantages. Different programming languages are used for different purposes and for solving different kinds of problems. Therefore, before developing a system, a programmer should have ample knowledge about the facilities that programming language provides, as well as the limitations of a programming language. Usually, it is considered that the first language to learn is the hardest for new developers, but as soon as they learn other computer programming languages, this process becomes easy.

Chapter 5

Best Practices for Developing Applications

Despite having the necessary knowledge about a programming language and its use, a programmer needs to learn about the best practices for developing the applications. The application development process is very innovative and creative. This process involves a lot of brainstorming and collaboration to create a successful product in the end. Different kinds of practices are utilized for developing applications. These practices should be followed to get a great product. As most of the population use smartphones nowadays; therefore, more and more application developers are creating new and innovative applications to fulfill the needs of the users. Quality applications are the need of the current IT industry. Following are some of the best practices that should be utilized for developing quality applications to fulfill the up-to-date demand for innovative and creative applications:

- **Knowing About the Audience**

It is very necessary to have complete knowledge about the target audience and users of the system. Without knowing the audience of a system, a developer cannot make a perfect system. Every developer should know about the target audience and learn about the features that are required by the audience. It is very beneficial to ask these questions right at the beginning of the software development process. It will ensure a smooth development of the system. Knowing about the audience will tell about the preference of the audience, and it will help to create a useful software product.

- **Creating an Understandable Application**

The application which is to be developed should have a proper purpose. The application must be meaningful. The application should be easy to understand by the general audience. Instructions must be available for the audience to completely understand the features of the application. The proper manual should be given to the end-users to use the system effectively. A proportion of graphics and text should be available in the application to make the application useful to the end-users. All the functionalities of the system should solve the problems of the users. A balanced and consistent design is the key to success in case of developing a useful application program. Creating a coherent and consistent application that fully conforms with the business user requirements is the key to success to create successful applications.

- **Selecting the Right Method of Application Development:**

Different kinds of software development methods and technologies are available to develop an application or software. Among all these different methods and tools, selecting the right choice is very integral for creating the application or the product successfully. A proper design strategy is essential for creating different applications. The design strategy will explain the different aspects of the system and the different requirements of the system. Using a proper storyboard for the entire team to understand the system completely is essential. The complete functionality of the system should be written down. All the components and features of the applications should be explained individually and properly. The developers of the system should understand the functionality with all its aspects. Great graphics and visual aids should support a good idea to make the program more useful and understandable. It is also very beneficial to include the end-users in the brainstorming and storytelling phase. The users will tell the developer team about their expectations and their requirements. The application designers can incorporate all the feedback into the main strategy of the system. By using the best model that will suit and fulfill the requirements of the user, the project will be taken on the right track. By using appropriate tools and techniques, the product will be finished in time and within budget.

- **Focus on the Development Phase**

The development phase of any application or software is known as one of the most important phases of the whole application development lifecycle. It is very necessary for the developers first to develop the core application functionality. It is necessary to develop the important features of the application first and then moving onto the least important features of the application. Sometimes there are additional functionalities that are required, and these functionalities can be provided to the users in the form of updates and upgrades. The core functionality matters to the users. Therefore, most of the time should be devoted to the development of the core functionality. In some cases, the first release of the application consists of the most important features of the application, and later, the upgrades are available in the kind of different upgrades and updates. In some circumstances, the users can even purchase new functionalities that are introduced later in the application, but firstly, it is the responsibility of the developers to provide the core functionality to the users.

- **Securing the Application Properly**

Nowadays, most people use the facility of smartphone applications. The mobile phones are susceptible to multiple latest IT threats. Nowadays, many applications are available over the Internet and the application stores. The users download these applications according to their requirements. Sometimes, during the downloading process, an unsecured application could cause a security threat to the mobile phone and the personal data of an individual. Therefore, mobile phone application security is one of the top priorities of IT companies currently. Users must be aware of digital threats and dangers. Everyone should know about the basics of application security and security techniques. Every mobile phone user should use appropriate security measures to stay protected over the Internet. Nowadays, most application developers devote their time to the security of the applications. Due to many cyber threats and cybersecurity vulnerabilities, most of the software development teams try their best to secure the applications appropriately. A software development team must utilize the best practices and the best tools and technologies that are available for securing the application so that the data of the end-users can be protected, and they can be saved from data theft and data loss.

- **Testing the Application Appropriately**

The testing phase of an application begins after the development of the application. The testing of the application is usually done before the release of the application. During the testing phase, the application is tested properly for its functionalities. The functionality of the software system is matched with the software requirements specification documents. A correct system conforms with the user's needs. It is very necessary to check the application properly. Nowadays, the development teams have dedicated individuals known as the testers who are responsible for testing the functionality of the system appropriately.

Testing is used to make sure that the system is working appropriately according to the requirements or not. Sometimes, the end-users are also involved in the testing of the application. The users will test the application, and they will check whether the application is working appropriately or not. After using the system, the end-users will give their feedback to the development team. The development team will utilize this feedback to improve the system for the users. Sometimes, the feedback also suggests some changes to make the application or software more user-friendly. The development team takes all these feedbacks into account, and the system is changed according to the requirements. The feedback of the end-users greatly increases the usability of the application.

- **Using Application Analytics Within an Application**

Usually, mobile devices are connected to the Internet all the time. In some cases, the applications work without any Internet connection. In this case, the mobile phone application developers usually use mobile phone application analytics to check the user behavior regarding the application. The analytics are incorporated into different applications to comprehend how the users are using the application. It will give a detailed insight to the application developers about the behavior of the application and the features of the application, which are used the most by the users. Sometimes, different kinds of application crashes are also recorded, and this application crashing information will help the application developers to improve the application in the future. The crash log information is one of the most important application features provided by the analytic application. It provides detail about the sequence of events that occurred in an application before the crash.

- **Incorporating a Feedback System Within an Application**

The feedback of the end-users is immensely important regarding the working of the application. The mobile application developers and software developers usually incorporate the feedback system within the applications and software. In this way, the feedback is recorded, which is given by the end-users. Usually, the users are given a social media platform to record their feedback appropriately. By using the feedback system within an application, the end-user experience is greatly improved, and the technical support is also increased. The feedback will also help the developers to fix the issues and design the upgrades according to the requirements of the users. By using the feedback system, the developers will have an insight into the most desired features within an application by the users.

- **Researching the Idea of the Application**

For an application to be successful in the market, proper research must be conducted before building the application. A lot of factors need to be analyzed before creating an application. It is very important to create an application that has an audience. If there are no users for an application, the application will be useless, and it will not generate any revenue. Understanding the audience is very important regarding the application. It is very important to learn about the different recommended features and the desired functionality that is needed by the end-users. It is important to consider how the application will facilitate the users in their real life. It is necessary to learn about other competitive applications in the market. In this way, the developers can devote their time to improving the features of the application and introducing such features in the applications that are relatively new and innovative.

- **Building Progressive Web-based Applications**

Progressive web-based applications are the key to success nowadays. These kinds of applications help to minimize the gap between web applications and native kinds of mobile applications. At present, most of the applications which are generated by using web-based application development languages provide native experience to the users. The user experience is greatly improved by using such technologies. By creating progressive applications, the native features can be easily utilized in a mobile device. Google recommends building progressive applications, which are key to building applications for the future.

- **Integration of a Rapid Content Management System**

Different businesses must incorporate a good contact management system for their website and applications. A proper contact management system is the key to success for business or corporate. The content management system is used to manage all the content effectively and efficiently regarding the company. The content management system provides a lot of features to the administrator. An administrator can use the features provided by the content management system to maintain the applications and websites. The application's functionality, content, features, users, and the graphical user interface can be maintained by using a content management system. The content management system also secures the content of a company for the future. The content management system is usually integrated at the time of development for a company or corporate.

- **Using a Proper Typography Technique**

A great software interface can be considered as the essence of the software development process. A captivating graphical user interface will attract more clients. Graphic designers have the key responsibility of creating captivating graphical user interfaces. More and more effort is exerted in the typography of the application. All the headings, subheadings, and titles present in the application are arranged properly according to the requirements. Special attention is given to the typographic techniques to make the application more useful and increase the efficiency of the application.

- **Selecting the Platform Properly**

In the present IT industry, three platforms are very common. These three platforms include Android, Windows, and iOS. While designing the application, it is necessary to select the platform properly. The programmers and the system designers develop the applications separately for every platform. A different number of techniques are required for programming in either of these three platforms. For the android based applications, the android studio is used.

Similarly, for windows-based applications, visual studio is utilized. For the iOS-based applications, the swift platform is utilized. It is essential to select the right platform for any application. Selecting a correct platform will give a detailed insight into the number of devices that the users will use. This detail will be beneficial to estimate the number of users regarding the application. It will also highlight the usability of the application and the popularity of the application among the customers. Selecting the platform for the application development process is a big decision. Selecting the right platform is usually the decision of the development team. The development tools are utilized according to the selected platform.

- **Application Design Considerations**

Application design is known as the backbone of an application. Typically, during an application development process, the application designers must design the application according to the requirement specification documents. But nowadays, the developers also must keep the check over the design considerations. The application developers must design the application according to the requirements. The application design will be in correspondence with the business requirements. Communication is essential among application designers and application developers. The application designers and the application developers must be on the same page regarding the application designing. The whole application development team must understand the requirements of the application. The application development team will develop the system according to the requirements. Different kinds of design elements are considered during the application design process. Selecting the design elements per the business needs is very important.

- **Considering the Different Features of the Application**

An application typically consists of a lot of features. The application designers and developers must prioritize the features according to the requirements. Usually, the most important features are developed first. The application developers move from high priority features to the low priority features. Sometimes, the developers and the designers of the application also consider the user feedback regarding the working of the application. Based on the customer feedback, the application developers and designers will design the high priority features of an application first, and then they will move towards the low priority features. The core functionality of the application is developed initially. Different kinds of plugins are installed in the last process of the application development process. Utilizing the plugin in the last step will make the application lighter and it will greatly increase the performance of the application.

- **Considering the User Experience**

The consideration of the product, along with a great user experience, will mark the success of the application. A great user experience is essential for the success of the application. In the final stage of the application development process, the application will be released over different application stores. The users of the system will download the applications from the application stores. In the last step, the application will be used by different users and it will provide a user experience. Mobile phone applications provide great speed and convenience to the end-users. Most of the population uses mobile phone applications nowadays to get convenience from them. Providing good user experience must be prioritized while developing the applications. Great user experience comes with a lot of benefits. Excellent user experience increases the popularity of the application and it also increases the revenue of the application. Providing great user experience and facilitating the end-users is the main goal of the application development process.

- **Taking Customer Feedback into Consideration**

Every application that is developed contains a section that includes the feedback of the end-users. Sometimes, the feedback also comes from the beta testers. The beta testers are involved during the testing phase of the application development process. In the testing process, the feedback of the system is considered for improving the product and making the changes before the release of the product. Sometimes, the feedback section is also given in the application, which is released over the application stores. In this case, the feedback is taken into consideration and the improvement of a system is made in the form of upgrades and patches which are released over the Internet from time to time to improve the application periodically. In some scenarios, the feedback is taken into consideration for getting the perspective of other users. Customer feedback gives the opportunity of testing the feasibility, efficiency, quality, and usage of the system from other user's point of view. Therefore, customer feedback is very important regarding the working of the application.

- **Developing the System According to the Application Store Guidelines**

Ultimately, the application will be released over the application stores to be available for general public use. There are certain rules and regulations regarding the use of application stores. An application should follow the guidelines and the rules that are set by the application stores before releasing them over the application stores. Sometimes, not following the rules of the application stores result in a rejection of the application from the application stores. If an application is rejected from the application store, then this application cannot be published, and it will not be available to the public. To save time and increase the speed of the development processes, it is essential to include the guidelines and make the system according to the set principles that are defined by different application stores. Apple application store and Android application store have its own certain guidelines that should be followed while publishing the application.

- **Including Accessibility Features in an Application**

Usually, the applications are developed to fulfill the requirement of the general public and people with perfect health and no issues. Sometimes, there are some special needs of people with disabilities. To accommodate the requirements of such disabled users, the application design should include certain accessibility features. In this way, the application will become famous among the disabled audience. With the advancements in technologies, numerous different kinds of tools and technologies are present to facilitate the disabled people properly. Certain features such as voice recognition, sections, virtual assistants from different applications, etc. will accommodate the needs of the disabled population.

- **Future of the Application**

The application development process is a continuous process. Once when the application is released over the application store, the application is continuously improved with the help of different updates and patches. Every application requires continuous maintenance for making it successful in the long run. An application is improved consistently and continually. Application maintenance is a very costly process that requires a lot of money. But, planning for the maintenance of the application in the earlier stages of the application development process can save a lot of time and a lot of resources for maintaining the application. An application should be developed in such a way that accessing it and changing the features is going to be an easy process in the future. The application maintenance and continuous improvement ensure that the application will work fine, and it will always perform greatly. An application should provide consistent and improved user experience continuously. Continuous maintenance and improvement of the application will ensure that the customers of the application are always happy. An application should be improved in such a way that after an upgrade or an update, it will relate back to the earlier stages and the earlier versions of the application. In this way, the users of the system who use the previous versions of the application will get the same great user experience as those customers who are using the latest versions.

- **Taking the Stakeholder's Expectations into Account**

The final end-product must behave according to the expectations of the stakeholders. Stakeholders are directly affected by a software or application development process. Stakeholders usually include investors, clients, and users of a system. If a delay comes during the development process or if the system does not behave according to the requirements, then the stakeholders will be affected. It is necessary to keep stakeholder's considerations and expectations into account. The stakeholders will only accept the system when the system will work according to their expectations and standards. Therefore, the system should behave according to the demands of the stakeholders.

Chapter 6

The Programming Process

The general programming process includes the conversion of a problem into a solution in the form of a computer code that is given to the computer. Programming is a very innovative process. Different instructions, which are given to the computer, are compiled by the compiler, and different kinds of tests are carried out to ensure that the instructions are working properly or not.

The programming process consists of six steps. These six steps are:

- Properly defining the problem.

- Planning for the solution to solve the problem.

- Designing the system architecture.

- Programming or coding process for solving the problem.

- Testing the program for its effectiveness.

- Properly documenting the program or code and maintaining the code.

The details of these steps are as follows:

- **Properly Defining the Problem**

This is the first step of the programming process. In this step, different kinds of users and stakeholders are also involved. The stakeholders usually meet the design and development team to define the problem. The application development and the application design team will consider the problem, and they will define the

46

problem accordingly. System analysts are required in this step to analyze the problem effectively. Different kinds of inputs that are required by the system and the outputs which are produced by the program are also defined in this step. At the end of this step, a written agreement will be present. This written agreement would include different kinds of business requirements, different kinds of inputs and output produced by the program. Defining the problem effectively is a very important process. This step will form the base for all the development processes of software or application.

- **Planning for the Solution to Solve the Problem**

This is the second step of the programming process. The basic goal of programming and coding processes is to offer the solution to different kinds of problems that arise for the users. This step will provide the main purpose of the programming. Different kinds of tools and techniques are utilized in this step to evaluate the solution and propose a perfect solution to meet the requirements of the user. Different kinds of flowcharts are designed to design the hierarchy of the program. Different kinds of pseudocodes are also written in this step. Sometimes a combination of both the pseudocode and flow chart is utilized. Both techniques will give a graphical description of the solution. Both techniques will provide a step by step guide for the application designers and application developers to understand the solution effectively. This step can be considered as the creation of the map, which is used by the design team and the development team to create a solution from scratch successfully. Different kinds of decisions and all the steps which will be involved in the application design process are highlighted in this step. All the other users can easily understand the pseudocodes and workflows. Any person who is not technical can also understand the pseudocode and workflows by simply looking at them. The pseudo-codes and workflow diagrams are written in plain and simple English language.

- **Designing the System Architecture**

After planning the solution for solving the problem, the designing phase of the application or software begins. In the designing phase, the design team of the application development works. The system designers will analyze the system. Different kinds of UML tools and techniques are utilized in this phase of development. The complete architecture of an application or software is designed in this phase of the application development process. Different kinds of diagrams, such as class diagrams, use case diagrams, system architecture diagrams, ERD's, sequence diagrams, and system diagrams, are generated in this phase of the development process. The design team of the application development process is responsible for creating such diagrams that will be forwarded to the development team later in the development phase. The development team will get the blueprint of the application from the application designers. It is one of the most integral phases of the application development process. The application design team must have a keen eye for all the functionalities of the application and this team will create such diagrams that will conform to the original software requirement specifications of the users. The design phase of the application will create the blueprint of the application and all the documents that will be created in this phase will be incoherence with the user business requirements which were designed initially during the start of the project.

- **Programming or Coding Process for Solving the Problem**

This step of the application development process involves the implementation of the system. This is one of the most important phases of the application development process. This step can be considered as the backbone of the application development process. In this phase of the development, different programmers and coders will utilize a variety of different programming languages and techniques to create the application or software according to the requirements. The development team will be involved in this step. The development team consists of different individuals who will be skilled and expert in using different programming languages and techniques for developing the system. The entire team will work together by using a variety of different tools and techniques to get the desired implementation of the system. This step is the most important in the application development cycle because this step is directly involved with the creation of the project. Without using a proper programming language, a system cannot be generated properly.

- **Testing the Program for its Effectiveness**

After generating the program for an application or software, it will be tested for its usability and quality. Sometimes, different kinds of bugs and errors are encountered by different programmers. To solve these bugs and errors, a software quality assurance team is essential for ensuring and safeguarding that the application will be free of bugs and errors, and it will perform its required work according to the requirements. The quality assurance engineers, and the application testers are responsible for testing the usability and the features of the application. Testing a program for its effectiveness is an innovative process. The testing of a program is repeated several times in the testing phase. After creating the intended program, it will be tested on its platform or device. The debugging facility is provided by different compilers automatically. Debugging an application shows that the application is working smoothly or not. Debugging also shows us different kinds of errors and bugs that are encountered in an application. In some compilers, different suggestions are also provided to the end-users. These suggestions help the programmers to correct the code and maintain their usability. Different kinds of errors are encountered during the testing phase. The translator program is used for checking syntax. If a syntax error is present in an application, then it will be highlighted by using the translator program.

- **Properly Documenting the Program or Code and Maintaining the Code**

Documenting a program is an essential process. This process is usually ongoing. Documentation properly describes the system and applications. Documentation correctly describes the entire application development life cycle. For any software or application, the documentation describes the following sections in detail according to the requirements:

- Description of the problem.

- Proposed solution.

- History of problem.

- Flowcharts.

- Pseudocodes.

- Content management.

- Database design.

- Programming language.

- UML designing.

- Sequence diagrams.

- Activity diagrams.

- ERDs.

- Class diagrams.

- Business cases.

- The functionality of the application.

- Test cases.

- Quality assurance.

- Management criteria of the application.

Sometimes after the release of the product in the market, the designers and developers must release an upgrade of the system. The upgrades are released during the maintenance of the application. In such scenarios, it is crucial to utilize the documentation. Properly documented systems require less time to fix the issues as the proper documentation is already available. Programmers can visit the documentation at any time they need to, and a software development team should have a system documentation expert who will document all the necessary details regarding the working of the software project.

Chapter 7

Best Programming
and coding Practices

During the application or software development process; usually, the development team works from scratch to build a system. Sometimes, the development team must work with the existing code that is previously available for utilization in an application. Some of the best programming and coding practices are as follows:

- **Using Consistent Code**

Any software or application project, despite its size, utilizes a programming language. For any program that the development team creates, they should use a consistent style of development. A consistent style of development has many benefits in the development phase of the application. As different programmers work on different parts and different features of the application, therefore a consistent style is essential for merging the different snippets of the application together. There is no right or wrong style regarding the application development process. Using a proper style and proper indentation for programming is essential for working between different projects and working between different team members. A consistent style of coding is essential for the success and long-term maintenance of the project.

- **Using Different and Unique Code Blocks**

Any code or any block of code should not be repeated in an application. Every block of code should be unique, and it should serve a purpose. Programmers should use consistent and coherent programming practices, and all the code of the application should be meaningful. The programmer should use the best programming practices and utilize a small amount of code that can be changed according to the requirements. It is one of the best practices not to repeat a block of code again and again. For any application, the programming should be clean and consistent per the user requirements.

- **Preventing Deep Inner Connections in a Program**

Sometimes, according to the nature of the different tasks and features of an application, it is necessary to use interconnections within an application. This interconnection ensures the linking and communication between different features that are interlinked together. Sometimes, this nesting and interconnection are essential for merging the different features and getting the desired results in the form of the application. It is recommended that most of the programmers should avoid deep nesting for creating clean code. Sometimes, due to the deep nesting and connections within an application, it becomes difficult to read the code, and understanding the code also becomes difficult. If deep nesting is present within an application, then the maintenance of the application becomes extremely hard for the programmers. It makes the task of maintainability of the application very difficult. Therefore, it is recommended that the application programmers and coders should utilize the practice of using clean and neat code and they should avoid the connections within an application wherever possible. Simple connections are recommended within the working of an application. A deep connection is recommended to be avoided for getting a coherent piece of code at the end of the development process. Deeper nesting can make the program extremely difficult to understand and comprehend.

- **Limiting the Amount of Source Code**

For the programmers that create great innovative and captivating applications, it is recommended that the programmer should use a small code. The code should consist of all the meaningful syntax and meaningful programmer practices. If the user's desired functionality can be achieved by using different functions and libraries in a short amount of length, then creating programs with a large length is not recommended. A good programmer utilizes the best programming skills to shorten the amount of code. If the length of a program is minimum, then maintaining the program will become very easy. The program also becomes easy to understand, and the readability of the program also increases in this way. If the program uses correct syntax and meaningful functions, the code becomes coherent and consistent. Therefore, small lines of codes should be utilized for programming purposes.

- **Giving Special Consideration to the Graphical User Interface**

The end-user will only see the screen of their mobile phones and other user devices. The users are interested in using the graphical user interface the most. It is essential to ensure that the application is user-friendly. The concepts of human-computer interaction should be taken into consideration while developing the application or software. All the components of the screen should work properly. It is vital to ensure that all the graphical components work together seamlessly and appropriately. Special attention should be given to the end-user controls. All the controls should work effectively, and they should serve their intended functionality correctly. The design team will be responsible for designing and elaborating on the main design of the application. The designer will design the size and positioning of every component on the user screen.

- **Work Saving Locations**

If a programmer is working on a problem or a project, it is recommended that he should save all his work in one single file or folder. This file in which all the work is saved must be easily accessible within the computer. A programmer should not save his work in more than two files because it will break the structure of the application, and the application readability will decrease significantly. A program must be saved in a secure location within a computer. This location of the computer should be backed up on the cloud with the help of other tools. This location should not be accessible to any other user out of the system. Keeping all the work in one secure location in a clean format is essential for working securely on an application within a computer.

- **Using a Proper Naming Convention**

Whenever an application is created, it requires a name. All the other users will use this name outside of the system. The name of the application is very important regarding the readability and correct definition of the application. Special attention should be given to the naming conventions to create a neat and clean code. All the variables and other programming items that are used within the application must be meaningful in their syntax. In this way, there will be less confusion when other team members review the application. It will make the code highly readable, and it will increase its usability and maintainability.

- **Simple Logic Design of the Application**

Every program or application requires logic to create it. Programmers or coders use this logic to create meaningful applications that are highly innovative and effective in their usage.

Every program should be designed with simple logic. Creating programs with complex logic will increase the complexity of the application greatly, and this kind of code will be difficult to be understood by different team members. It will be difficult to maintain the application and reuse it in different cases. Using simple logic to create neat and clean blocks of code is essential for creating a successful product that will meet the desires of the users and provide the solution to problems.

- **Make the Code Readable**

When a project is created, different members of the development team are involved in its making. One developer will create a block of code, and another developer will develop another block of code. Overall when the whole project is merged, then the entire team will work on it together. Therefore, it is necessary to make the code as simple as possible and it should be readable and understood by all the developers (nickishaev, 2017). Optimization of the application comes after the readability of the application. If an application is difficult to read, then a lot of time and a lot of resources will be spent over understanding it properly. Therefore, optimization comes at the second number and the priority is given to the readability of the application first.

- **Special Attention Must be Given to the Application Architecture**

An amount of time must be spent over creating the architecture of the application. The practice of coding without knowing the application architecture is entirely useless. If programmers start working on a project without its architecture, then a lot of times, a huge problem comes in the last phases of development. A lot of resources are spent to fix the things at this stage. Therefore, proper planning must be done to create the system architecture properly. Every member of the development team must understand how the application will behave and what is the proper functionality of the application. The entire development team must understand the proper knowledge about the modules and services of the application. Connecting a comprehensive architecture is the key to success while creating different kinds of applications. There should be a separate design and architecture team that will be dedicated to creating the architecture first. This design team will forward the architecture of the application to the development team and the development team will work over the architecture to create the desired functionality according to the user needs.

- **Planning for Future Updates Carefully**

Whenever an application is released over the application store for general use, it will be updated continuously. The application development process is only the first step in the development phase. An application is continuously improved to maintain the quality of the application. Different kinds of errors and bugs are fixed in the updating process of the application. An application is continuously improved for improving the customer experience regarding the application. New features can also be introduced by using the updates of a system. Therefore, system updates should be maintained properly to make the application successful in the future. The developers should have a keen eye regarding the updates for an application.

- **Providing a Personalized Experience to the End-Users**

Nowadays, many applications use personalized experiences for end-users. The data scientists keep track of user insights to know about their preferences. In this way, personalized experience is provided to the end-users. If users get personalized experience in an application, they will download the application more often, and the users will use the application happily. Personalized experiences greatly increase the popularity of the application and the revenue of the application among the users. Therefore, most of the application developers currently utilize the option of personalized experiences within an application to facilitate the users according to the requirements.

Chapter 8

Important Elements
of an Application

Regarding the working of an application, many important considerations should be considered. Numerous mobile phone applications are available over the play store. An application should have certain key elements to perform well in the application store and to be successful. For every application, there is a very competitive market where similar applications are also available. Therefore, for an application to be successful in the long run, it should have certain elements to make it stand out in the crowd. Here are some of the key elements and their details which different application developers should use to make their application captivating and provide best customer experience regarding the working of the application:

- **Simple Design**

An application should have a very user-friendly interface. For an application to be successful, the design of the application should be simple, and it should facilitate the users to navigate different features of the application easily. Design from the customer perspective. All the controls of the application should work well with speed. The design process of the application development process is very integral for this phase. The end-users require a very simple application to work effectively for their purposes. The application can be very complex, but the functionality provided by the application should be simple with a user-friendly interface. In this way, the application will be successful among users.

- **Standing Out in the Market**

For an application to be successful in the marketplace, it should be available for a variety of different application platforms. This means that the application will be available over all platforms such as Android, iOS, and windows. If an application is not available for all the platforms, then there will be a reduction in the number of prospective clients. As more and more people are migrating towards the mobile phone application development, therefore the application should be available for all the platforms. An application should perform well in the market to be successful and generate revenue for the development team.

- **High Performance Regarding the Working of the Application**

Nowadays, more and more applications are developed every single day. These applications are getting better with great performance. It is imperative to create such an application that will perform very well on all levels. The users of an application do not like an application that is slow in its working. An application should have a faster loading time. The cache of an application should work very quickly to provide high performance and fast loading time. It is also very essential to quickly update the application for any errors or bugs to optimize it for new upgrades and new features. Therefore, high performance regarding the working of the application is essential.

- **Security of the Application:**

New applications are created every day; therefore, new security breaching techniques and threats regarding the security of your application are also developing at an increased rate. Data is one of the most important elements of a user. It should be the priority of an application to make the data of the end-user secure and protecting the data from external dangers and security threats. At present, many applications use different kinds of payment methods to facilitate application purchases etc. Therefore, it is essential to secure the payment methods for the end-users and securing the data transfers regarding the payment systems is very imperative. At present, many applications are developed for the health care industry.

Regarding these health care industry applications, it is essential to secure the personal data of the people. Many companies use customer insights to gain valuable data regarding the most in-demand medicines and medical techniques. It is very important to secure the personal data of the individual regarding their health. This sensitive data should be protected. Therefore, the security of an application should be the top priority of the developers.

- **Providing Personal Features to the End-Users**

Most of the users nowadays like to use the customize features of an application. These customized features are tailored according to the needs of the users. In the mobile applications, different kinds of special content are generated to fulfill the demands of the users along with customized forms and different themes of the application. All these techniques will facilitate the users to utilize the application more often. This technique is one of the best techniques which will leave a positive effect on the customers regarding the application (Desai, 2018).

- **Data Analytics**

The field of data analytics was introduced along with the field of data science. Better analytics provide detail insights into customer and user behavior. For any mobile phone application or software, the data analysis techniques will show the preferences of the users and the most desired customer functionality. In this way, many companies and businesses can improve their business applications. By using the data insights and the valuable data from the techniques of data science, the application developers can create such innovative applications that will be in most demand by the users.

- **Integration of Social Media**

Nowadays, more and more people are using social media for sharing content over the internet. Utilizing social media integration for any application is very important. Different kinds of social media platforms are linked together over an application. It will facilitate the signup process for the users. This feature will provide the facility to the users to create their account from any social media account of their choice. It also facilitates the sharing of information in a great way. By using social media integration, the application can become popular very easily. Open media integration is very important nowadays, and it facilitates the users greatly. Therefore, every application that will be deployed over the application store should use social media integration.

- **Avoiding Excessive Clicks and Taps in the Application**

Every application that will be deployed over the platform must be very easy to use. To make the application navigation easy for the users on any internet connection, the developer should avoid unnecessary clicks and tabs for navigating between the different sections of the application. A clean screen should be provided to the users. A simple graphical user interface will ensure that the user will stay on the same page for a lot of time. Most of the users do not like moving from one place to another a lot of times in an application. Therefore, to facilitate the users regarding the working of the application and making the navigation easy, it is recommended that a simple interface should be provided to the users with the minimal number of clicks and taps for navigation purposes.

- **Maintaining Relevancy of the Content for the Application**

In some cases, sometimes, the business applications are made after the web application development process. These applications offer content regarding the business in the form of an application. It is imperative to provide relevant content on the mobile phone that is in correspondence and in coherence with the website. For any business, applications that are rich in their content and the content which is relevant to the company will ensure the success of the application. Mobile phone applications are intended to represent the business to the end-users. Therefore, the mobile Phone application should be relevant to the website of the business or corporation. For many businesses, the relevant application which provides the desired functionality to the users can mark the success of the business.

- **Device Orientation Should be Kept in Mind**

While designing the application, the device orientation should be kept in mind. The target device must be taken into consideration. The target device orientation will help in the designing of the application. According to the requirements, the design of the application will be adjusted as either a portrait or landscape view. Sometimes, both views are designed simultaneously in the application. It is an important consideration in the design phase to design the proper orientation or the application.

- **Excellent Image Resolution**

The screen of the application must fulfill the requirements of the users. Providing users with an excellent image resolution will increase the user experience. Providing the users with a high-resolution screen will increase the user experience greatly, and it will increase the worth of the application. Nowadays, more and more mobile phone application manufacturers are using high-resolution screens. Therefore, to cope with the latest developments in mobile phone screen resolutions, more and more developers are developing high-resolution mobile phone applications. The graphics of any application needs to be high resolution and high definition along with a lot of color schemes that are available to make the application captivating for users. Therefore, color schemes and themes should be selected appropriately with a high-resolution screen. All these things will make that application useful and it will increase the screen time of the users by using the application.

- **Providing Search Option to the Users**

The searching option is one of the essential options that could be present in an application. The searching option will enable the users to navigate the different sections of the application. The users can also utilize this option for searching the Internet. Integrating this option inside the application will greatly increase the usability of the application. This feature is usually not required in the game-based applications, but this feature is useful in utilizing different business applications and different social interaction-based applications.

- **Excellent Color Schemes**

The graphics and color schemes can be considered as the backbone of the application. Every application should consider different color schemes and themes that will attract more customers. Nowadays, more and more complementary colors are also being utilized for creating different kinds of applications. Using a proper color scheme and a theme of an application will make the application beautiful and professional. It will increase the usage time of the applications greatly.

- **Using Push Notifications Within the Application**

Nowadays, this a trend of using push notifications within an Application. Push notifications can have any form such as text, picture, or a combination of a text and picture. Providing personalized push notifications will increase the popularity of the application. The push notification should be relevant to the users and they should not be general. By using push notifications, the users can be made interested in certain actions regarding the application. An application must use push notifications to make it more useful.

- **Considering User Feedback**

Considering the user feedback is essential in an application. Feedback will make the application very successful. Review and feedback are essential for any application. The users of an application can provide adequate feedback to improve the application in ways that the developers and development team cannot understand. A section must be present in an application where the users can record their feedback appropriately. Feedback is known as the perfect way to know how customers feel about the application. By using the feedback of the users, an application can be improved greatly, and the worth of the application will be increased automatically. By simply placing a feedback button, an application will collect unlimited feedback by numerous numbers of users of the application. In this way, the clients will better understand the system and they will increase the usability of the system by providing different opinions regarding the usability of the application. Feedback is very imperative in an application for getting user attention in an application.

- **Updates of an Application**

After considering the feedback of the system, the developers will plan the update of the system appropriately. In this way, the updates will be released for the system. Feedback will show how more relevant content can be shown to the users. The developer team will carefully create all the updates of the system by considering the feedback. By using updates, a better product will come into existence with improved functionality. Updates will make the system get a clean look and feel. Updates are released periodically for any system. Updates are an essential part of any application.

Chapter 9

Fundamental Parts of a Program

At the very core, programming can be considered as working with different kinds of building blocks. These building blocks are joined in a different order to get the required functionality. Different kinds of blocks are merged, and new blocks are created to get the desired effects. Overall, all the different programs consist of five main elements. The details of these elements are as follows:

- **Input**

In real-life scenarios, the input can come from anywhere. Different kinds of keyboards that screen, files containing different texts, etc. are some common examples of input devices. Input is an important element of a program. Input is required by a program to perform different tasks. Input is required for the processing of different functions within a program. Every program is based on some logic in which the input is taken from the users and different kinds of processing are done over the data. This processing is required for the main functioning of the program. Therefore, the input is an integral part of every program.

- **Output**

The output is commonly known as the result of a computer program. Every program produces an output or a result. This result is required as the main goal of the program or code. Every program is designed to produce the desired result. The result of a computer program, which is the output of the program is usually saved and presented to the user over a screen. The main aim of the programming is to create the desired results and outputs based on the user input. Every program produces some output based on the inputs and the arithmetic operations that it is set to perform.

- **Arithmetic Logic**

Arithmetic logic contains all the logical processing within an application. Arithmetic operations such as addition, multiplication, division, subtraction are performed with the help of arithmetic logic within an application or a source code. Mathematical logic facilitates the logical processing of different objects and variables within a program. Arithmetic logic can be considered as the backbone of the logical processing within a program. The programmers usually consider a logic first and then apply the logic with the help of different arithmetic operations. As the computing power of the computer is very large, therefore a lot of arithmetic logical operations can be done in a single step within a program.

- **Conditional Statements**

Sometimes, different decisions are taken within a program. For making different kinds of decisions, a combination of different conditional statements is used. A variety of different conditional statements are present within the different programming languages. These conditional statements are utilized according to the requirements. Some common examples of conditional statements are IF, IF-ELSE, WHILE and DO WHILE conditions. Conditional statements make the decision making it very easy for the developers. The decision is imperative in any programming language. Therefore, conditional statements are utilized with several different data structures to fulfill the needs of the situation.

- **Looping of Different Statements**

Sometimes during the working of a project or a program, certain statements need to be repeated and again. The looping structures provided by different programming languages are used for looping between different statements again and again. Certain conditions are present where the programmers can stop the iteration of different loops when certain conditions are met. Different kinds of loops are present in programming languages. The looping structures are used in different programming languages for meeting the requirements of different scenarios provided by the end-users. Looping structures are one of the fundamental utilities provided by different programming languages. By using the computational power of the computer, different programmers use multiple loops for their desired functionality. One of the most famous loops is known as the FOR loop. Some of the other loop examples include the WHILE loop and DO WHILE loop. One common example of the looping structure can be considered as follows: Suppose that the programmer wants to run a statement five times until a certain condition is met. The programmer will use the for loop which will iterate five times. When the condition is met, the loop will break, and the output will be presented to the user.

Chapter 10

Basic Elements of Source Code

Programmers create a program to generate source code. A human being easily understands source code. The file where all the programs are stored is known to have the source code. Source code comes before a compiled version, whereas the object code comes after a compiled version of the program. For some programming languages, there is usually one form of code. For generating source code, different tools are utilized. These tools include notepad, compilers and integrated development environments. Different kinds of tools are present with integrated development environments to manage different states of a single program.

Some source codes are free of cost, whereas some source codes require a proper license for their use. Another kind of source code is known as proprietary software. In the case of proprietary software, the source code is not shared with the users, but a usable portion is shared with the users to fulfill their demands. The proprietary software has an intellectual property associated with it; therefore, it cannot be modified or changed by an individual.

The open-source software is designed for making the code public to the users. This sharing of the source codes depicts the collaborative efforts of developers. The open-source software is enhanced and improved by many developers simultaneously. A lot of people are associated with the source codes. The primary purpose of source code is to provide customizable installation of the system to the skilled individuals. Source code can also be used by other developers to generate similar programs with desired functionality. Allowing access to the source code benefits the entire software community. The code is shared among different individuals, and the code is improved among different developers.

Computer programs or the source code also differs between different programming languages. The proper syntax is followed for the different programming languages, with all source code being translated into the machine language first. This language is understood by the computer. The compiler performs all these language conversions. The output of the source code is stored in the file known as the object code. The object code consists of a special format that is not easily understood by different developers. An executable file is generated by using the object file. This executable file will perform all the functionality of the desired program.

In the present fast IT industry, different kinds of source code management systems are present. The programs that help the developers to create their desired source code effectively and efficiently. These programs greatly support the source code generation process. These source code management systems support the collaboration of different programs at a single time very easily. The teamwork capability is one of the greatest capabilities provided by the source code management systems. Source code is known as the main essence of the programming language. The main goal of a programming language is to create source code for providing a solution to an existing problem.

For any source code, different kinds of libraries are utilized for performing a variety of different functions. These libraries are built-in for use in a program. Different custom-made functions are created by programmers to get the desired functionality in a program. All the components of a program work together to get the intended output of an application. The input, arithmetic logic, loops, and conditional statements work together to produce the required output, which will solve the problems of the users.

Chapter 11

Benefits of Learning to Program or Code

A lot of benefits are associated with learning how to program effectively. These benefits are present equally for new programmers as well as experienced developers. There is a perception that is associated with programming, and this perception usually shows that programming is the work of smart minds only. Nowadays due to advancements in technology and the latest innovations, by using social media effectively, anyone can learn how to program or code in his favorite programming language. Anyone can become a programmer and use his skills to become successful in the field. Following are some benefits of learning to program or code:

- **It makes Programmers Think in a Smart Way**

The programming skills greatly increase the thinking capability of the programmers and coders. In this way, this programming skill can benefit individuals in other fields of life as well. The main goal of programming is to solve the problems of the end-users. Usually, a very big problem is converted into smaller parts, and the smaller parts are solved individually. This problem-solving capability helps the individuals in real life as well.

Regarding programming, the programmers create a set of code which is understood by the computers and they use logic to create a working program. A proper mindset is developed by using the coding and programming practices, which helps the people to solve the problems, and the problem-solving capability increases greatly by using different kinds of programming languages. The programmers can learn any new concept easily and they can solve any new problem by using the brainstorming techniques.

By learning to program, the programmers can understand that they can solve any problem no matter how much size and extent it has. Before creating any code, the programmers usually think first about the possible solutions. The program must present the possible solution and then define the use cases according to the requirements. Programming produces effective and efficient systems by using analytical and quantitative skills. By solving different programming problems, the motivation of the programmers' increases, and they tend to move towards other bigger problems and their solutions. Therefore, the most important benefit of learning programming is increasing the problem-solving capability not only in the computer world but also in the real-life and real-life scenarios.

- **It Positively Impacts the Career of Different Programmers**

Programming is known as the field of the future. There is always a great demand for programmers in the IT industry. Programming is a bright career choice. If a person works hard in the programming capabilities, he can make a successful career very easily in the software industry. A lot of opportunities and carrier choices are present within the programming industry. Several different areas of specialization are present within the software and computer science industry. A person can become a programmer, system designer, requirement elicitation specialist, application manager, etc. The person only must learn how to program, and he can then select his carrier further by learning other specialized techniques. A person can help the design team as well as the development team at the same time if he has designing capabilities as well as development capabilities. It is recommended that the person should learn to code from verified sources.

Several different courses are available over the Internet, and a lot of books are also present from where a person can learn how to code. By using a proper course or a teacher for learning, programming can help the people to make a full time IT career easily. The demand for programmers is always very high. A person only must Polish his skills in the necessary programming languages and software development techniques, and he can certainly make his career. It is necessary to learn those programming languages which are high in demand and not focusing on such programming languages and techniques which are obsolete at present.

Sometimes people can move from being an application designer to an application developer. By switching between different branches of the application creation process, a person only must learn new skills. Opportunities are present for him to move and switch from one field to another. One of the most important benefits that is associated with learning the programming languages is the ability to work as a freelancer. A person can work as a freelancer from his home as there are plenty of opportunities present on the Internet where a person can select the product of his choice and work on it according to his own time and schedule. This opportunity of working as a remote freelance developer is one of the most highlighting capability provided by the software development and application development industry. Anyone can increase his problem-solving capability greatly by making new programs and learning about new techniques and innovative processes that can help solve the problems. Learning about programming and coding is an ever-continuing field, and this field has a very bright future. It is one of the most highly rewarding career choices out there.

- **A Competitive Salary for Programmers**

For almost all the people in this world, getting financial success is the main important aim for them. By learning how to program, many people can get financial success nowadays. It does not matter what the background of the people is or what their profession is; a person can learn to program at any time of his life. There are plenty of opportunities by which a person can make the most financially by using the opportunities provided by the application development profession. Programming skills can also allow a person to make his carrier individually. Many application developers do their own business and create different kinds of websites to become successful. Different kinds of startup founders are working solo currently. Coding skills are essential for becoming a successful entrepreneur and a successful startup founder. The earning potential is very great for programmers and coders. They get competitive salaries in the IT industry. The demand for programmers who are skilled in their field is ever increasing. Programming is a bright career choice.

- **Improves Social Life**

Learning about different programming skills can improve the social life of individuals. It changes the way people think about other people. Different programmers use that capability to make applications and websites for the people they care about and facilitate them by creating beautiful products for them. In this way, a person can increase the worth of his social connections. Learning about programming can improve the social life of people greatly. A person can utilize his programming skills in any way to improve and maintain a social life.

- **Improves Creativity and Brings New Ideas to Life**

Programming provides the capability of shaping ideas into reality. All people have some dreams. To bring dreams to reality and giving a real perspective to the dreams, programming helps the individuals to shape their lives. A variety of different tools and techniques will be available to the end-users to give their ideas a real shape. The capability of working remotely by using different internet-based techniques enable the freelancers to work from anywhere around the world. Any person can learn how to code by using a very flexible schedule. A huge amount of data resources available over the internet, which can facilitate the people to learn the latest techniques and innovations regarding the IT industry. A person can work personally on a project by using his own schedule. Any user can match his imagination and shape it into a reality by using the programming and coding techniques. In this way, a person does not have to convey his entire idea to other development teams. He can create the system himself and enjoy it according to his own demands.

- **Increases the Self-Confidence of the Programmers**

After accomplishing and creating a certain program, it provides immense satisfaction to the creator. This feeling of self-confidence is one of the most accomplished feelings in the world. Any person can create great things by using programming and coding capabilities and create many different complex systems. If a person knows how to code, then he can become empowered by using his capabilities in a better way. One common example of this scenario is that if a person creates a website from scratch, he can create his own design and make his dream website according to his imagination and desires. This user does not have to rely on the templates and building material provided by other users. When he creates all the products and services by himself, he no longer must use the skills of other people. This will give him immense satisfaction and improve his capabilities. Any person can develop more confidence by using coding and programming techniques and interacting with the

Internet. Whenever a person solves a technological issue, his self-esteem and confidence increase greatly (An, 2018).

- **Improves Computational Capability of the Programmers**

Computational thinking is the process that provides the users the ability to show their thoughts properly and logically. This process is very similar in its working as that of writing different instructions that are used for coding on a computer. This is a problem-solving capability. This method of computational thinking is used by different programmers to solve real-life problems. Computational thinking involves different concepts that include mathematics, logic, and algorithm. Usually, a problem is broken down into different sub-parts which are small and single steps are taken to deal with the problem at hand. These steps are solved in a logical order which works effectively. The programming concept of abstraction is also involved in this process. In the abstraction method, a child class can be moved from one class to another, and the child class can be utilized generally between the program. The computational capability is one of the best capabilities to be learned by the developers and the development team.

- **Programmers become more Efficient Productivity Increases**

Any programmer can utilize his skills in the field of computer science and create a usable and proper piece of code. The benefit of using computers is that they can do the tedious and repetitive work efficiently and effectively. Different programmers utilize this capability to achieve their desired functionality. Sometimes, programs require a lot of time for their processing. A lot of resources are required for performing tasks. In such cases, the power of computers is utilized. Different kinds of productive and sensible tasks are accomplished by using the power of computer systems. By using different programming structures, a lot of tasks can be automated automatically. This automation facility saves a lot of time for the programmers. The time required for solving tasks also decreases greatly by using proper programming languages.

- **Communication Skills of the Programmers and Coders Improves**

For any programming project, a lot of people are involved in the programming team. Different people of the programming team have a different perspective of looking at things. Regarding the programming project, every member of the programming team will have a different level of experience and understanding regarding the working of the project. To deliver a software project effectively, different members of the software team will work together and collaborate. If a programmer has thoughts about a project, he can communicate his thoughts on the project effectively with other colleagues. A person will become very confident about the working of the project if he knows the technical side of the project. A programmer can discuss the implementation details effectively, along with programming and coding practices. The value of an employee will increase if he knows how the programs behave. Communication skills between programmers increase greatly by learning coding and programming skills.

- **It Provides a Firm Understanding of How the Software Works**

By using different kinds of programming languages, a programmer can get a firm understanding about different kinds of devices that are used in software development, different kinds of software development environments, different kinds of tools that are involved in the creation of different software, and different technical tools that are required in the whole application development process. In this way, if a person learns how to code and how to program, he can become very familiar with the basic software development tools and techniques that are highly recommended in the digital IT industry.

Every person who wants to have a solid background with the application development and software development processes must understand all the different tools and techniques which are required in the software development process.

- **Combines Creativity with Technical Skills**

Software development is a very technical process. The software development and application development process require different levels of technical expertise to gain the desired effects. There are very few fields in which there is a combination of proper technical innovations along with the creativity of the programmers. Application development is such an innovative process that combines both skills at the same time. The process of coding is all about identification of a problem properly and then highlighting different kinds of solutions and making a proper system that will conform with the user needs. Therefore, techniques are developed to solve the real-life problems of the users in a better way of getting the desired effect.

- **Creates an Online Presence**

The current digital age in which people live nowadays, it is very necessary to create an online presence. In this way, if a company or a business will Google an individual or a business, if it is available on the Google search results, then authentic credibility is present for that business or company. Online presence is very important in technologically driven industries. Creating an online presence is a mandatory tool for managing different kinds of employers and businesses nowadays. It is essential for different kinds of businesses and companies to list themselves over Google and maintain their name online. To create an online presence, many companies and websites nowadays create their own websites to manage their name online; if an individual wants to create an online presence for himself, then he will start with a personal blogging website.

- **Starting a Personal Business and Becoming an Entrepreneur**

After learning the necessary programming and coding skills, A person can open his own E-Commerce store. In this way, that person can create his own business and sell the products according to his desires. There are numerous other ways in which a person can create a business by using technical skills. A person can create his own online publication. An online shop can also be created and maintained. A web-based design agency can also be created. A person can make his own company on time and facilitate the creation of mobile phone applications; a person can also teach other people the coding and programming skills by becoming a teacher online. A person can also earn revenue online by reviewing different products and writing a detailed review about them online. There are almost endless options available over the Internet for any person to earn his income. The methods mentioned above are known as some of the most common methods of earning revenue online.

- **Creating a Personal Time Schedule**

Nowadays, there is a trend of becoming a freelance developer and self-employed individuals. A person can spend his time to learn about the necessary coding and programming skills, and then he can utilize these skills to become an independent freelancer. A person can work remotely in this field. In this way, a person will work according to his own schedule. A person can also hire other people to do his job. It does not matter where the person resides because working is independent of his location. In this way, learning about different programming and coding skills will give the users the freedom of choice and the programmers can manage their own schedule and work remotely from anywhere in the world.

- **Getting the Benefit of Self-Learning**

There is continuous progress in the field of application software development. Due to this reason, a person can have a competitive

81

benefit in self-learning. A person can learn about programming skills by working on numerous exercises himself. Numerous resources are present over the Internet for learning about different programming languages and learning about the working of different applications and software. If a person is a professional software developer, he needs to find new ways in which he can solve new problems all the time. This learning process is continuous, and this process is ever evolving. It is necessary to understand the different new topics which are utilized in programming and system creation tools. A person should understand the big picture of a problem. In this way, he can create and design different innovative solutions. A person can handle numerous kinds of practical projects to become successful in the future.

Chapter 12

How Programs are Created

Computer programs are generated everywhere nowadays. The presence of computer programs can be felt in every machine, which is around users these days. The world is becoming very digital these days. Different people are generating different kinds of ideas and programmers are implementing those ideas to create applications and benefit the users greatly. Every person has some ideas regarding some useful applications. To get a detailed insight into how different programs are created, Following is the detail of the application development process:

• **Generating an idea**

Different kinds of programs are generated to facilitate the users greatly. The current software industry is based on certain tasks that are performed to facilitate the users. Performing different processes in the form of programming can make life easy for users. The main goal of creating a program is to provide users with a proper utility. Therefore, it is essential before creating an application to create a great idea. It is necessary to keep a check on all the daily tasks which a user performs. Examining the daily task, a person can figure out which tasks need automation and other tasks that can be made easier by using an application. In this way, a great idea can be created. It is necessary to generate proper detail with the idea so that proper design can also be created for the idea, and it can be shaped into an application for the future.

- **Examination of Other Similar Programs that are Available in the Market**

Several different applications are already present over the application stores. The Android, Windows and IOS Platforms have their own application stores. New applications are available over the application store for the general downloading of the users. the users typically download the applications from the application stores, which are native to their platform of usage. To develop an application and make it successful, it is necessary to locate such applications that have similar functionality. By examining such applications, a programmer can get the idea about the demand of the applications and which kinds of applications and features are the users require. By examining similar applications, a programmer can comprehend other features that are required in the application and how he can make the application more unique and useful to the users. Typically, new applications are developed every day with additional features and such features that are not available to the users before. By examining other similar programs, the programmer can get a great idea about how he can improve his application greatly in the marketplace.

- **Writing a Proper Design Document for the Intended Application**

The design documents are known as the backbone of the application development process. Regarding the application development process, the design is involved in designing the system effectively. The design team will create the application design documents, which will outline all the basic functionality and the main goal of the project. The design documents are typically forwarded to the development team during the application development process. Great and consistent design documents will help the development process greatly and it will keep the project in coherence with the user requirements. Several guides are present over the Internet for creating different kinds of design documents. The design documents help to achieve the project on time and on budget. The design documents also highlight different kinds of UML designing patterns. The designing of a system consists of many kinds of diagrams such as activity diagrams, sequence diagrams, use case diagrams, and workflow diagrams. In the last phase of the design process, the programming language which will be used for the development of the project is decided. Some of the test cases are also designed in the design phase which will test the basic functionality of the application. These test cases will be further improved during the testing phase of the application. Providing a coherent and consistent design document is the key to success for creating a great product that will fulfill the intended functionality.

- **Creating Simple Designs First**

If a person is new to programming, then it is recommended that he should start the simple project first rather than taking complex projects initially. For getting hands-on experience with the programming languages, it is recommended to start with small-sized programs and then moving over to the more complex systems. Programming requires a lot of patience and time to getting better at it. Therefore, it is recommended that any person who is new to programming should create simple functionality of the application first, and by achieving the simple functionality, it is necessary to move towards achieving the complex functionalities later. It is also recommended to create the interface of the application first and designing the back end of the application later. More amount of time and energy is required for creating the graphical user interface. The graphical user interface is used by the users first; therefore, special attention should be given to its design. Different kinds of editors and compilers are available in the programming language. It is also necessary to start from a simple programming language first, which is easy to learn and use, and after that, using other more complex languages. For the first time programmers, it is necessary to download and use a code text editor. Some languages have built-in text editors and compilers. Whereas, for some languages, the text editors and compilers come separately. Learning an essential programming language is essential for creating applications with complex functionalities. By using the compiler or interpreter, a person can use high-level languages and design more complex features of a system. There are also some languages present for programming purposes which are interpreted languages. In these languages, a separate compiler is not required. These languages are compiled automatically as their system is installed properly on the computer. In this case, the application will run quickly just by a click of a button. Some examples of interpreted language which are used more often are Python and Perl.

- **Utilizing the Basic Programming Concepts in an Application**

Programming is known as a very innovative process. It matters greatly which programming language is selected for the design process. It is essential to understand the language and to understand its most commonly used concepts. It is necessary to program an application smartly. Using the basic concepts of programming, an application is mandatory to achieve the desired effects in an application. Every programming language uses a syntax which should be followed for avoiding the syntax error while writing code. Therefore, after selecting a language for creating an application, it is necessary to learn its syntax. Different kinds of concepts are also present in a programming language. These concepts make the application development process easier and these concepts also facilitate creating the applications by using the desired utilities and functionalities. Some of the most common concepts which are used in almost all the programming languages include:

- **Variables**

Variables are essential for storing different kinds of data temporarily in a program. Without using a variable, data cannot be stored, and therefore any logical operation cannot be taken over the data. In every programming process, the data is usually taken as input from the users and different kinds of operations and processing is performed over the data. The data is manipulated, altered and changed in many ways in a program. To create different processes and perform the processing over the data, it is essential to store the data in some way in the application. By declaring different kinds of variables, the data is stored properly inside a program or an application.

- **Utilizing Different Conditional Statements**

Based on different kinds of inputs and the data that is stored inside the program, different kinds of conditions are mixed and matched in the program according to requirements. Using conditional statements is one of the basic functions of using a programming language. By using different kinds of conditional statements, logic is implemented in the program. Usually, in a program, different kinds of true and false statements are considered. Based on these true and false conditions, different types of conditions are met according to the desired requirements. Every programmer should know how to use different conditional statements as the conditional statements form the basis of every programming language.

- **Using Loops for Different Repetitive Tasks**

During the processing of a program, it is recommended that certain processes are repeated several times. For facilitating this repetitive process, different kinds of loops are utilized in every programming language. The loops are present in a programming language for checking between a range of certain numbers and matching the conditions between the range according to the needs. By using the computational processing power of a computer, high-level applications are made which contain loops that run over a million times.

- **Properly Using the Escape Sequence Commands**

During the programming process, the programmer must know some basic shortcuts. These shortcuts make the life of a programmer very easy by performing certain tasks with the help of a single click. These simple commands include creating new lines, using indentations, commenting between different lines of codes, and performing many other smaller shortcuts. Using these simple shortcuts between the application development process will save a lot of time, which can be used for building the application properly.

- **Using the Comments Utility during the Programming**

Usually, an application development process involves an entire team that is dedicated to the development of the project. Many people will read a single block of code. To make the code more readable and make it easy to understand by the developers, it is a standard practice to use different kinds of comments between a normal application development process. Commands usually have two types. These two types include single-line comments and multiline comments. Different numbers of backslashes are used as a shortcut for creating comments. By using comments, the application developers describe certain lines of code in a human-readable language. In this way, if other members of the development team want to understand the system and the lines of codes, they can simply read the comments and understand the program very easily.

- **Reading Different Kinds of Programming Books**

Books are always known as one of the most useful resources for learning any programming language. The programming-based books are available everywhere around the local bookstores. Nowadays, programming-based books are also available online. Despite having a lot of material available over the Internet, a book is still a very invaluable tool. A book that is based on our programming language can have an unlimited amount of resources, which can help the programmers to get a deeper understanding of certain topics. It is a standard practice to read about different programming languages on the Internet and then consulting different kinds of books. The programming books usually consider real-life examples along with the behaviors of application and programs. These books can also sometimes depict the real-life functionality of the applications. The programmers can greatly understand the working of similar applications by using correct book resources.

- **Regularly Practicing the Programming Exercises**

A programmer cannot become a skilled programmer unless he regularly exercises different programming strategies and tools. It is necessary to get help from other experienced programmers and learn about new techniques. Without practice and making different kinds of programs, a person cannot get detailed insight into the programming concepts. Like every other field of life, programming can also be improved by using a lot of practice exercises. The more a programmer will practice different programs, the more experience he will gain.

- **Building a Prototype of the Application**

Building the prototype of an application is just like building a blueprint of the application. The prototype of the application will show all the basic and important features of the application in detail. Wireframing is known as one of the most important techniques for demonstrating to the users how the application will behave. In the case of wireframes, different kinds of patterns and usable tools are depicted on the mockup screen. The orientation of the application and the actions performed by different event listeners are also depicted in the wireframes. The wireframes provide the necessary capability of the system. Business cases are also useful in depicting the different users of the application and how the users will interact with the application. The prototype will alter according to the user requirements frequently during the project development phase. The prototype will depict all the aspects of the application. If the prototype is being made for a game, then the prototype should depict all the fun aspects of the game. All the important aspects of the application should be depicted in the wireframes.

- **Creating a Great Development Team**

The application development task is the task of a development team. An effective development team is essential for making a successful product in the end. All the members of the development teams must be involved in using different kinds of programming languages and different techniques that are used in the application development process. An application development team is essential for keeping the project on the right track. The development team will take the design documents into account, and the development team will design the application and system according to the user requirement specifications. Usually, all the applications are developed from scratch. But sometimes different programmers tend to use certain prototypes to develop features that are just incorporated according to the project requirements. By using the proper methodology of developing a system or application, incorporating the different changes which come during the later stages of development is easy to handle (How to create a program, 2019).

- **Testing the Application after the Development Phase**

After developing the product successfully, it is essential to test the project according to the user requirements. Usually, the testing processes are done by an entire testing team. Different kinds of testing are performed to ensure that the system is working properly or not. Different kinds of testing techniques are also applied to check the system for its functionality. Usually, a program tester is responsible for testing the software system and its quality. Typically, different kinds of inputs are used for checking the behavior of the system. Invalid variables are also used for testing purposes. For checking the graphical user interface and all the components that are present over the graphical user interface, the testers will click all the buttons and all the other graphic user interface components. The testers will check the behavior of all the event listeners that are present on the screen to ensure that every button and every tab is working according to the requirements. The navigation of the application is also checked properly. The tester will move between the different screens that are present in an application. An NDA (Non-disclosure agreement) is required during the testing of a commercial product. A testing plan is essential for testing the system appropriately. All the errors and bugs should be properly reported. Certain software can be utilized for the management of processes. A common example of such software is GitHub. GitHub is a management software that is used by different software developers to collaborate on a project. It is necessary to check the product again and again. Errors and bugs can come in any phase of software development; therefore, the prototype of the software should be checked again and again.

- **Solving the Bugs and Errors with their Priority Numbers**

The bugs and errors must be solved from a high priority level to a low priority level. Attention should be given to very high priority errors first and then moving towards low priority errors. The bugs are also solved based on their severity. Some bugs are known as the blockers. These bugs affect the normal working conditions of the program. The critical features are also checked during the testing process. The different bugs and errors that have high severity are resolved first. The priority of the bug shows the order in which the priority needs to be resolved. The errors are resolved according to the deadline of the project. Different errors delay the development process of the software. Therefore, the errors and bugs should be given special attention to be resolved as early as possible. All the features that are added are tested one by one.

- **Adding More Features in a Program**

In the alpha phase of the application development process, more new features are added to the program. At the end of the alpha stage, all the basic components will be present in the system, and all the basic functionality will be available in the design as well. The design of the system must be in coherence with the original design and development strategy. When new features are added, these features will be in coherence with the original design. More features are added in a system simultaneously.

- **Locking the Functionality of the Software System**

When the alpha phase is completed, all the features that are implemented are locked. Typically, all the features are locked after their implementation, and the development team moves out of the alpha phase of development. No further features are entertained after moving out of the alpha phase of development. All the features of the system will be in the working stage at this phase of development. The beta testing phase begins after the alpha testing phase of the development. Beta testing includes more testing and polishing of the final software product.

- **The Beta Testing Phase of Software**

This testing phase begins after the alpha phase of software development. In this stage, the program is generally available for a larger audience. If the beta phase is made public, then it is called the open beta phase of the development process. Many people will use the software system and test its functionality. Using open beta testing is the choice of the development team. If the project is highly confidential, then the beta testing will not be open but rather, it will be done within the confidential individuals only. As the development of the program advances, the program will become more and more interconnected. Especially in the case of distributed applications, the application or program must rely on the connections with the servers. In such cases, the connectivity is tested thoroughly, and the connection is also checked with a lot of network loads. This connecting will ensure how the system will behave once it is released to the public.

In the beta phase, more and more importance is given to increasing the usability of the application and improving the utility of the program generally. Creating a proper user interface becomes mandatory in this phase of software development. This step will ensure that all the added features are working properly or not. Linking the user interface with the functionality of the system is a very complex process. Designing the user interface also includes the concepts of human-computer interaction. Usually, a software design team is involved in designing the user interface of an application. During this entire process, bugs and errors are continuously searched and mitigated. By using the best technologies and techniques, the user interface is designed and developed. The user interface will consist of all the important features of the application, which will fulfill the requirements of the program.

- **Focusing on Finishing and Improving the Functionalities**

After developing all the core functionality of a system, developers and the development team will focus on finishing the product with perfection. All the functionalities that are developed in the previous phases of development are improved simultaneously. In this stage, more focus is present over improving the functionalities and making the system effective and creating such a system that will conform with all the basic user requirements documents. All the functionalities are polished further to improve and complete the program. Even during this stage, the bugs are continuously hunted down and mitigated. Testing the system at this stage will ensure that a clean and neat product will reach the end-users.

- **Releasing the Program for Public Use**

The end goal of creating the complete software system is to release the system to the public or the users of the system. For releasing the system, different kinds of application stores are available. The development team will release programs over specific platforms according to their designing of the program. Releasing the program for the public will make the application available over the smartphones or dedicated systems of the end-users. Different kinds of marketing strategies are also applied by releasing the product to get more attention and make the application or system more popular. Different kinds of advertisement techniques are also utilized in this process. At this stage, different kinds of marketing specialists and marketing teams are hired to make the project stand out among the thousands of applications that are already available on the application store. Different kinds of social platforms are also utilized to increase the popularity of the application. Different kinds of postings are done to make the program public. Different kinds of press releases are also utilized. The press releases are usually released over the technical websites. Technical websites are visited by millions of users every day. Therefore, by using press releases, the application and the software system will become very popular. Different kinds of Flyers and business brochures are also customized to make the application popular. All the social media platforms such as YouTube, Facebook, Twitter, etc. are utilized for creating the marketing and branding of the system. In the case of websites, websites are hosted so that they can become public. Generally, in the case of applications, the different application stores are available for releasing the product to the public.

Chapter 13

How to Maintain the Code

After creating a program, it is necessary to maintain the program effectively. Several different rules and regulations are present in different software development companies. These rules have defined how the code is made maintainable and robust. Usually, there are two steps involved in creating a project. These two steps include writing the code and then saving the code in version control software such as the "Git Hub." Whenever a particular system is developed with the help of a lot of developers, then managing the code can become a more difficult process. It becomes very technical to maintain the code effectively. When the work piles up due to the non-management of code, then it takes a lot of time to make the project come again on the right track. All these factors will greatly decrease the developer productivity. As a result, job satisfaction decreases greatly. Therefore, a certain set of rules should be implemented in the development environment to maintain the clean code and make the project as successful as possible. Some guidelines regarding the code maintainability are as follows:

- **Defining Certain Rules and Regulations regarding the Code Maintainability**

Whenever a new team member joins the development team, it is the responsibility of the senior software development engineer to tell the rules regarding the writing of the code to the new member. In this way, the new member can become familiar with all the new rules and regulations which are implemented in a certain software development environment. The rules and regulations typically involve certain kinds of conventions that are required for writing and maintaining the code. Some companies use predefined rules, whereas some companies use custom made rules to suit their demands and needs. For example, Google company have its own method of defining different kinds of code. The Twitter software uses the Scala software for maintaining the code. A certain team should be present in the software development environment to ensure the quality of the code. In this way, the quality of the code will be checked simultaneously, and the code will become more and more maintainable within a specific period. If a dedicated team is available for maintaining the code, then the development team does not have to spend more resources and time to maintain and fix the greater issues that arise during the software development process. Certain kind of effort is required to maintain the system effectively and to follow the rules. If a certain project code is developed properly, then it will create a great amount of job satisfaction, and the amount of time which will be needed to complete a system will increase and the efficiency and productivity of the development team will increase as well. It is necessary, therefore for every member of the software development team to follow the general guidelines and rules and principles regarding the maintainability and efficiency of the code.

- **Using Software such as Static Code Checker to Check the Amount of Static Code within a Project**

In some situations, it is difficult for the programmers to keep the check of the code and the lines of code they are writing. Therefore, different kinds of static code analysis tools are available in the market. These tools can be utilized within the programming environments. These tools analyze the software under construction, and then they will highlight the static code. They also highlight the different lines of codes that need to be checked and revised. Using our analysis tools within our software development process is a very efficient way of checking the code. Without compiling the code properly, these tools can show and highlight the weaknesses within the lines of codes. These tools are automatic. Therefore, these tools will highlight the weaknesses within the different programs effectively and they will save a lot of time. An easy way is present for different developers to follow different kinds of programming conventions and guidelines while using the static code checker and similar static code analysis tools. Using these tools is the best programming practice nowadays. It is usually a little hard to learn how to use this software, but once when they are utilized properly then the efficiency and productivity increase greatly regarding a system.

- **Reviewing the Code Effectively**

Several different ways are available to review the code effectively. Different companies follow different kinds of rules to review the code. Generally, this process is known as a general process, but it involves a lot of detail and energy to review a code properly. Reviewing code is a very important process. This process cannot be ignored during the development phase of the application. It increases the efficiency of the program and the quality of the program greatly. Reviewing the code have a positive effect on the entire program. Nowadays, it is a single dedicated field for different programmers to become the code reviewers. In this way, programmers can improve the quality and functionality of the application. Different kinds of business risks and logics are analyzed while reviewing the code. Sometimes, different code blocks are merged, and, in this way, the merger of the codes needs to be analyzed to make an effective system. In such cases, a code reviewer is very important within the software development process. After reviewing the code, the code is checked again and tested again for its effectiveness. Different kinds of testing techniques such as unit testing, integration testing, etc. are utilized for faster processing and checking the system again. Different kinds of peer reviews are also involved in the testing process. By considering peer reviews, the code is greatly improved. It is necessary to take the feedback of the code reviewers positively and improve the code according to the requirements. Code review is a critical process and it should be incorporated in all the development phases to make a smart system.

- **Writing what is Necessary for a Code**

Sometimes, different kinds of variables are created within the working of a program. It is necessary to name the variables properly and make the code meaningful. It only takes a small amount of time to properly name the different variables and data structures that are used within the application. The variable is used for different representations of values. Therefore, the variables should be named properly. Sometimes, the programmers do not give a lot of attention to the naming of variables and proper naming conventions; in such cases, when different errors and bugs come at the last stage of the development, then it becomes very difficult to maintain the code properly. All the code that should be written must be meaningful so that if another programmer reviews the code or see the program, then he can understand the program effectively. The code should be very clear to all the people within the development team.

- **Special Attention should be given to the Variable and Method Declarations**

It is a standard practice to declare the different variables at the start of the class. By using such an approach when these variables are utilized within an application, then a person only must view the top of the code. In this way, a person doesn't have to scroll down the entire program to gain access to the necessary variables. A program can contain even thousands of lines; therefore, a standard procedure should be realized for writing the variables at a proper place.

Similarly, if a variable need to be available in a method and it will be used only once, then using it as a local variable is an essential practice. By using different methods, different kinds of functionalities are achieved within an application. In this way, the method should be made meaningful and the method should be declared in such order in which they will be utilized later in the program easily. If a method is going to be called first, then it should be declared first. In this way, if another person reviews the code and views the code again, then it will be properly understood and maintained by other developers. Important methods are declared at the top of the class and minor methods are usually declared at the end of the project.

- **One Function to Perform a Single Functionality**

It is usually a standard practice that one function will perform only one functionality. If a method is required to perform 2 to 3 functionalities at a single time, then the function should be properly divided. The functionality should be divided into two functions. In this way, one method will be used to perform one single functionality. If a function performs only one function, this function will be very easy to understand. This function will be easy to utilize with other resources of the program. It is also standard practice to make smaller size methods. If a method consists of a lot of input and it produces more than one result, then handling the result and the inputs at the same time become very difficult. Using a small method will greatly impact the quality of the code, and the quality of the code will increase greatly.

- **Minimize the Amount of Code**

If a proper functionality can be achieved by using one line of code, then writing three lines of code for a single similar task is not a good practice. Best approaches must be utilized for writing the minimum amount of code. All the different blocks of code should be optimized for the best performance. By using the minimum amount of code, there will be fewer reviews by the code reviewer. The code reviewer will also ask to minimally refactor the code in case of the minimum amount of code. The duplication of a single block of code can greatly impact the code, and it is considered a very bad practice in the programming language. A method in a block of code cannot be reused. The different methods present between a goal should be made as universal as possible. The code should not be duplicated in any way. In this way, the best application or software can be developed. Best practice should be utilized while developing the code. Learning about the best development practices can greatly facilitate the development team. Using the best practices for development purposes can make the project successful and it will also increase the capabilities and skills of the programmers and coders.

Conclusion

We all live in a data-driven world of technology. Numerous technologies are available everywhere around us. In this digital world, software and computer science technologies are everywhere. Many people wonder how different technologies, software, and applications work together. Coding and programming are available everywhere nowadays. Becoming an application developer is one of the brightest fields currently. Different kinds of technologies and innovations are involved in the application development process.

Smart mobile phones are available everywhere. There are approximately 5 billion users of the smartphone in the world currently. A huge population is utilizing the smartphone for their daily activities. There are countless applications available over the application stores which provide great facilities to the end-users. There is a great advancement in the programming languages and application development technologies in recent years. The three most famous mobile phone application development platforms are Android, Windows, and iOS. In the early years, only a few programming languages were available which were very difficult to use for programming purposes. The last decade of the 20th century and the early years of the 21st century saw the progress and development of many latest programming languages such as Java, C sharp, and a majority of the web-based development languages. The innovation among the application development languages is continuous and this field is ever evolving.

The coding process can be considered as the basic backbone of the application development. Different programming languages and integrated development environments are utilized for creating different kinds of applications for smartphone users. An application consists of many important components such as a graphical user interface, a front end, a back end, third party supports, and plugins. Typically, an entire application development team is involved in creating a successful product. After the successful implementation of the program, the program is continuously maintained and upgraded according to the latest needs of the users.

The coding process and programming process are very important application development processes. The code is available everywhere around us, and its implementation can be seen in everyday activities. Different kinds of applications and software are developed according to the diverse needs of the users. Some applications and software are developed solely for supporting the business and corporate processes. These software and applications support different kinds of business processes; therefore, these software and applications are incorporated inside the business processes.

Without the basic programming processes, a computer cannot perform its basic functionalities. The concepts of coding and programming are essential. The latest knowledge about computer science and Information technology subjects is incorporated in the course of young students who are in their school. Nowadays, according to the present situation and computer technology that is everywhere, the young minds who are at the level of school are being trained in computer subjects. Learning about computer science and computer-related subjects can make young students eager to learn about the latest technologies, and it will help them in shaping their future as well. By incorporating the basic computer science knowledge in the study plan of young students, the young students can polish their programming abilities right at the beginning of the career and they can become sound and knowledgeable computer professionals in the future.

Computer programmers are responsible for creating the program logic, the backbone of any computer programs. This does require some brainstorming by the developers, though. Computer coding is a detailed process that involves careful designing, writing, implementing, testing, and maintaining the application or a computer system. A proper understanding of the programming languages is mandatory to create great applications and programs.

The basic purpose of the programming language is to solve the user problems and providing coherent and consistent solutions to the end-users. Any person can become a programmer by learning different kinds of programming languages and different techniques that are present for developing applications and programs. Programming provides the opportunity for individuals to shape their great ideas into reality, and the skills provide great flexibility regarding the working hours and schedule of the programmers. Programming is a great problem-solving process which involves the division of a big problem into smaller problems. The smaller problems are solved periodically. In this way, it provides the capability to the people to solve real-life problems as well as computer-based problems.

For becoming an effective programmer, a person must acquire hands-on experience regarding the field. During the programming process, many kinds of errors and bugs arise. The programmer solves all the bugs and errors periodically, and, in this way, he gets the correct understanding regarding the working and efficiency of the program. The problems that arise during the application development process are decomposed and solved one by one. This decomposition technique is one of the key features provided by the coding techniques.

In a program, different kinds of components work together to make a proper system. Different elements are involved inside a program.

Usually, a variable is used for storing different kinds of values in an application. As different kinds of data are required within a program, a variable is used to store different values in a program. Different kinds of decision-making operators are also involved in a program. The decision-making operators decide within a program whether a statement is true or false. For operating different kinds of data together, the utility of arrays and stack is utilized. The most important component of a program is known as the functions. The functions are responsible for the custom behavior of any program. Programming languages provide built-in as well as custom made functions. Different kinds of inputs and outputs are utilized within a program. The inputs are typically used for getting the data from the users. The program typically uses the input to perform some specific functionality for the program. The result after the processing of the information is presented to the users in the form of the output of the program. Usually, a file reader is used for getting the input from the user and the file writer is used for presenting the output to the user in the desired format.

A programming environment is essential for coding and compiling the program properly. Due to the advancements in the field of computer science, nowadays, a variety of different integrated development environments are present to facilitate the programmers to code properly. Different sets of tools are already present inside the programming environments to facilitate the users to get the desired functionality. The programming environments are typically downloaded from the internet and then they are installed over the computers. The programming environments are also available in the form of CDs etc. to install them directly on the computers.

After installing the programming environment, different kinds of programming languages are utilized to code a program effectively for different applications and software. The software development process is an innovative process, and it usually requires a team of software developers to complete a task with perfection. Every program starts with a basic idea. The idea is further refined in the planning phase of the development. Usually, an entire team of software development specialists is involved in designing and developing the product. The design team will be responsible for designing the documents of the application properly. The design documents are very important documents and the design documents will contain different UML diagrams that will help the design of the application.

The UML designing will include the complete architecture of the application or software. The UML design documents will include different kinds of use case diagrams, activity diagrams, sequence diagrams, flowcharts, pseudocodes, business cases, and wireframes of the application or software. For the back-end development purposes, the UML diagrams will provide different kinds of ERD diagrams that will depict the efficient working of the databases that will be involved in the back-end development and the data access processing in a software or application. The application development team will be responsible for taking the design documents into account and then developing and implementing the system according to the requirements of the users. The main goal of software development is to provide efficient solutions to the end-users and provide the necessary solutions which will be in compliance with the user requirement specification documents. During the development phase, design documents are considered again and again to map the system according to the exact design of the intended system.

The testing phase of the application begins after the development phase of the application. A quality assurance team is responsible for maintaining the quality and testing the system properly. the system will be checked thoroughly for its working and its efficiency by the testers. Different kinds of testing strategies will be applied to test the effectiveness of the program properly. If certain bugs and errors are encountered during the testing process, then the system will be forwarded to the development team again, and the developers will remove the errors and bugs. The main goal of the testing process is to ensure that the system is working properly, and all the functionalities are in conformance with the user or business needs. Some famous software testing strategies include unit testing, integration testing, black box testing and white box testing techniques etc. Testing is known as one of the main processes of the application development cycle.

After the complete implementation of the system, the system will be released to the public for general use. Different application stores are available for different platforms. The three most famous platforms include Android, iOS, and windows, and these three platforms have their own application stores over which the programmers will deploy the applications. In the first step of releasing the application over the application store, the programmers upload the ready version of the software over the application store, and the application store will check the content of the application for any malicious or dangerous code. After passing through the verification process, the application or software will be released to the application store for general use.

The phase of maintenance of the application begins after the release of the application. The maintenance of an application is a continuous process. An application is maintained by releasing different kinds of upgrades that include the desired functionality, which is recommended by the users. The program is released over the application store once and it is updated regularly and periodically.

Maintenance of an application is a very technical and important process.

Regarding the code creation process, certain guidelines need to be followed to create a great end-product. These guidelines will ensure that the code will be coherent, and it will be reviewed a few numbers of times by the code reviewer. A code reviewer is responsible for reviewing the code. Typically, in the last phase of the application development cycle, a code reviewer will review the code and notify about the required changes to the development team. If the code reviewer finds that the code is not consistent, then he would ask the developer team to review the code again and making the code more consistent. To save the code from more changes at the later stages of development, it is necessary to follow certain rules regarding the code creation.

The code should be useful and meaningful in its working. Code should be smaller in size, and all the content of the code must be coherent. A single block of code should not be repeated. A static code checker software must be installed while working on a program. This static code checker software will ensure that unnecessary code will be removed according to the program features. It is also a standard procedure that all the methods that are used within an application are defined first at the top of the class. The functions are defined in such a way that they are periodically used later in the program according to the order of their presence. The variable and method declaration must be given special attention. All the variables and methods must be properly described with appropriate syntax and meaningful names. In this way, if another team member who is associated with the development of the code reads the code, then he can easily understand the meaningful variables and methods. It is also recommended that the amount of code should be smaller so that the code can remain consistent and coherent. By following the proper guidelines of creating a meaning code, the process of maintaining and updating the application in the future becomes an easy process. These guidelines facilitate the working environment for the programmers and make the coding process a simple and innovative process.

Application and software development are very innovative processes. These processes require a collaborative effort from all the team members that are involved in the development of the product. Project development starts with proper planning. After the planning phase, brainstorming is done to create different kinds of solutions for facilitating the end-users. After the brainstorming phase, the design phase of the application development begins. The design phase provides necessary documents that are used by the development team. After the design phase, the development phase begins. All the project implementation is done in the development phase. After the development phase is completed, proper testing and quality assurance management of the application or software is done. After all the phases of the development, the product is released for public use. After the release of the product on the application stores, the application is maintained constantly for providing great user experience to the customers.

Creating efficient programs is a tricky process. The programmers should learn how to create coherent and consistent code by following different naming conventions and programming guidelines. A program or code should be created by keeping in mind the checklist, which is used by the code reviewer while reviewing the code. In this way, minimum mistakes will come during the testing phase of the product and the product will be released over the application store in short amount of time.

A lot of benefits are associated with clean code. Writing a code is such a process that it needs continuous improvement. If a code is complex in its nature, then it would be very difficult to test properly. Any type of testing would become difficult if the code is not clean. As majority of the software testers use automated scripts in order to test the code, if a code will be complex then it would be difficult to automate the testing process. Clean code is very easy to test, and it also helps in faster diagnosis of the problems that are present in a code.

Numerous resources are spent over the maintenance of a software system. If a code will be clean then minimum resources will be spent over its maintenance and more time will be spent over the actual implementation of the product. With clean code, the maintenance become a very easy process and it becomes a less expensive process.

A clean code consists of different number of blocks. These blocks work together to achieve the desired functionality. For a clean code, a single block of code can be modified, refactored and read easily by other team members that are present in the development team. In the case of clean code, the code blocks can be altered easily without changing the entire source code. Programmers who edit the code in such cases have more confidence over the alterations at are required in the application.

The code is well defined in its functionality if it is clean. All the interconnections within an application are also defined properly. Programmers can completely understand how changing one part of the application will effect the other features of the application. The errors and bugs are also well defined in the case of clean code. Since the code will be very simple, therefore, more complex errors will not be hidden inside the code complexity of the application. The mistakes in the reasoning and the logical part of the program will also be more visible.

The developers who work with the clean code are more satisfied with the working circumstances of their job. They work with less complexity that is present within the programs. This scenario in the longer run increases the job satisfaction and professional satisfaction of the programmers. Clean code ensures that the code will be highly focused on the reader. A clean code is a written block of code that is easy for humans to understand.

A clean code is highly efficient and it provides great maintainability as it is focused not only on solving the problem but it also fixated on following the proper architectural style of the code. A clean code provides a proper flow of the application between different classes and functions of the program. A well-defined flow of the application is visible by using the clean code.

During the development of a project, the code is made as clear as possible. The programmers focus over the logic of the application that is utilized in the programs. All the activities of the application, techniques and patterns within an application revolve around the basic logic of the program that provides a clean solution to the user problems. Clean code provides a standard foundation for all the other team members that are present in the development team. It provides a quality standard to all the programmers.

Using a simple code will not complicate the problems that are present in the typical software development environments. The features in an application should be added according to their necessity. If a features requires an upgrade in the next two years then incorporating this upgrade at present is not necessary. The programmers cannot predict the future of an application. Therefore, the features of the application should be added according to their present requirements and needs rather than focusing over the future of the application.

A code must utilize proper indentation within its architecture. Proper indentation will increase the readability of the code greatly. The programmers can easily search the different components within a program by using indentation. Using appropriate naming conventions also help to achieve such a code that is easily editable in the future. Utilizing proper indentation and naming conventions in a code will provide great consistency within a code. Reviewing a code that is consistent is very easy.

By using consistency, simplicity, proper logic, clearness within code, proper indentation and naming conventions, a cost effective strategy is achieved in the program. A clean code will greatly decrease the cost of development. As the code will be simple and easily readable, therefore less resources will be spent over the maintainability and quality assurance of the application. A reader centric code will be available as the end product and this is the essence of the software development process.

References

Admin. (2018, November 28). Your quick guide to the history of coding.

An, E. (2018, January 11). Seven benefits you will notice when you will learn how to code.

Basics of Programming. (n.d.). Retrieved from Tutorial point.

Desai, A. (2018, June 6). Key elements of a successful business mobile application.

Hackernoon.com. (2019, January 31).

How to create a program. (2019, November 4). Retrieved from Wikihow.

nickishaev, A. (2017, January 9). 13 simple rules for good coding.

www.ingramcontent.com/pod-product-compliance
Lightning Source LLC
Chambersburg PA
CBHW071226050326
40689CB00011B/2471